The Infinite Imagination

Adult Coloring Book Vol.1

About The Artist

I grew up in an artistic family and have been an artist ever since I was a little girl.

At 17 years old I had my first professional art gallery exhibit. Later, I studied Architecture and Interior design, with my specialty being furniture and lighting design.

Over the years I have created hundreds of paintings and designed many products, such as, dog toys and clothes, furniture and a skin care/cosmetic line.

"I believe art transforms our emotions and opens our visual awareness".

Bereniche Aguiar

Art and Shop Website: www.berenicheaguiar.com

Recommendations

I recommend only using colored pencils to prevent any color bleed through on the pages. I also suggest putting a piece of cardboard underneath the page being colored, for more support, if it is desired to press hard with the colored pencils.

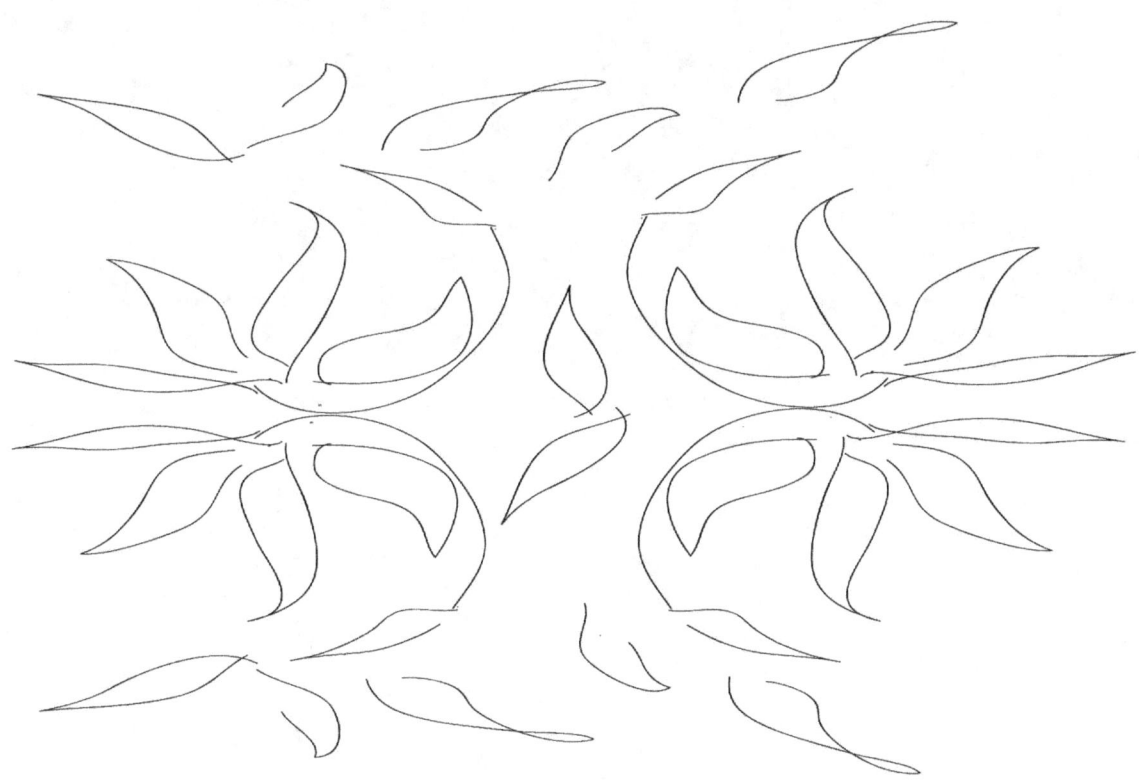

The full size drawing is on page 76

D# 2

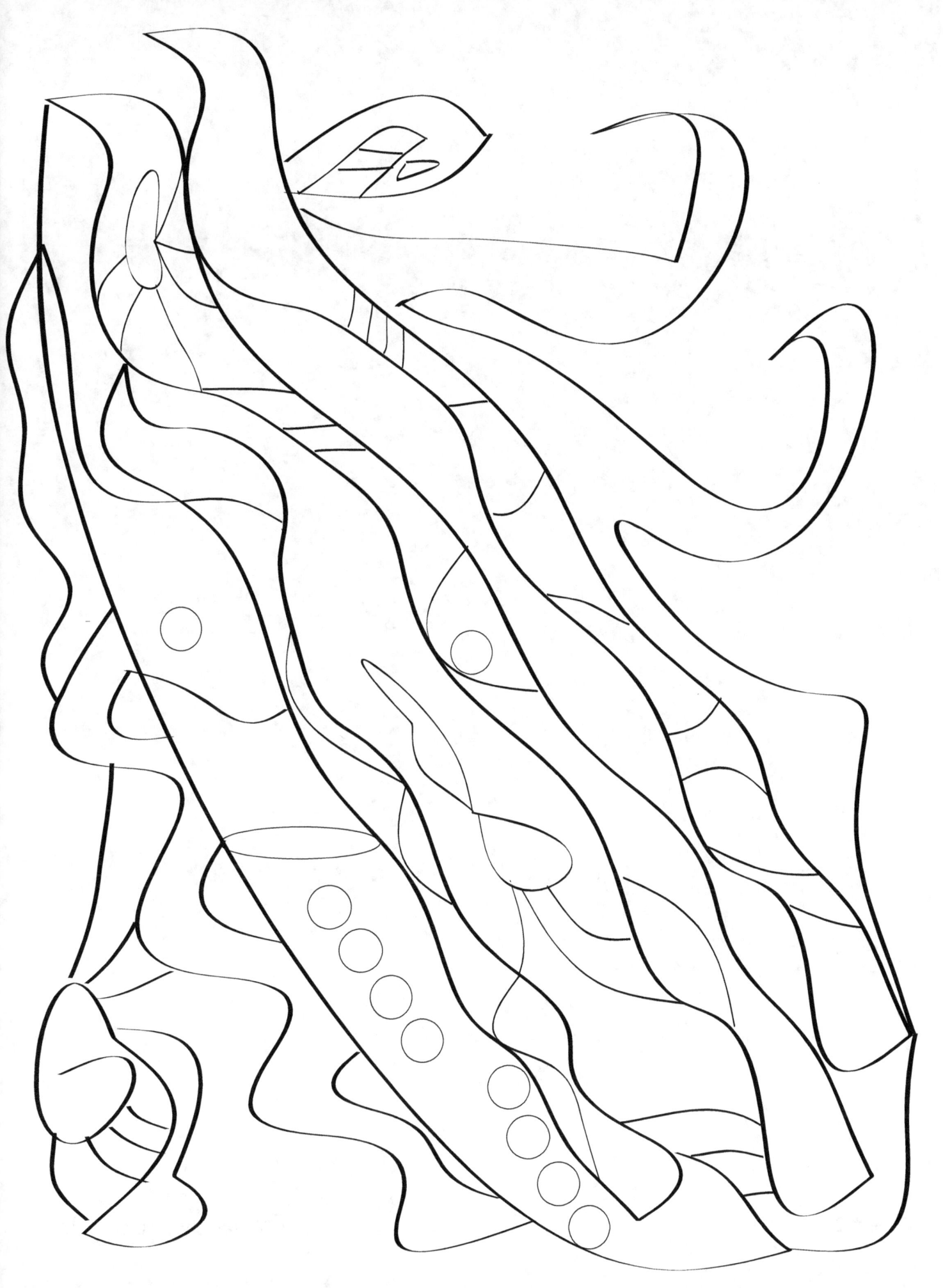

D# 1

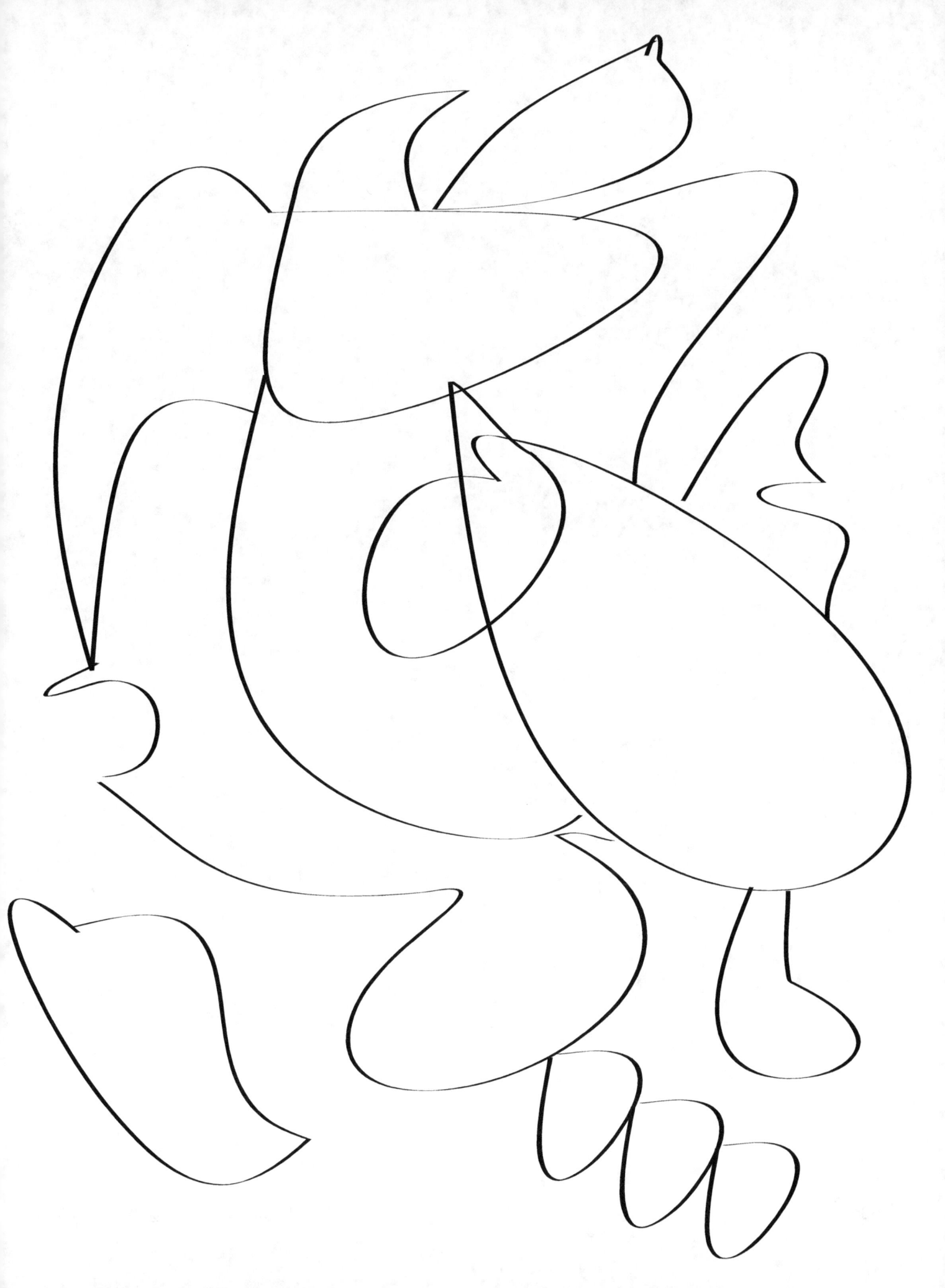

D# 190

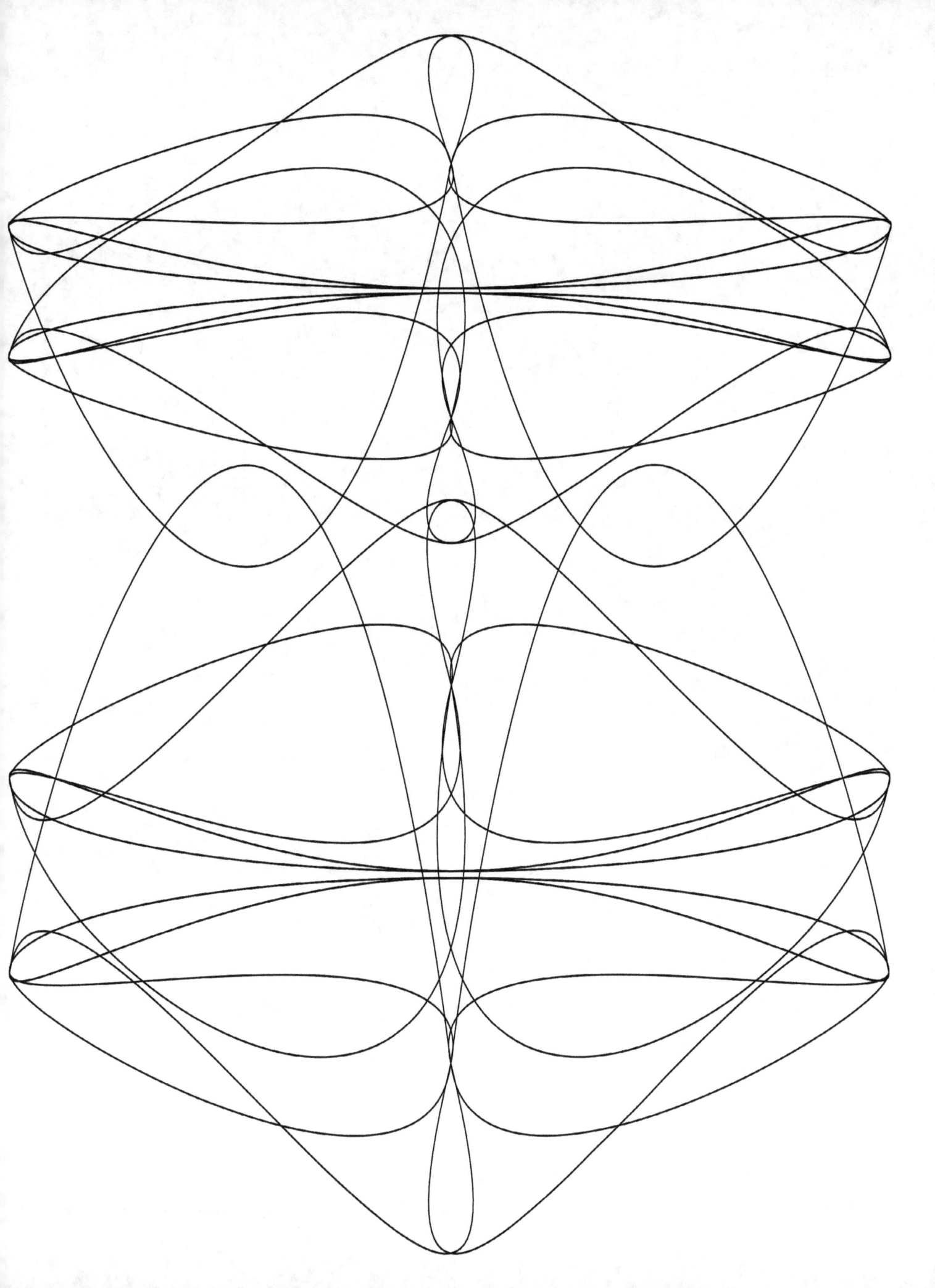

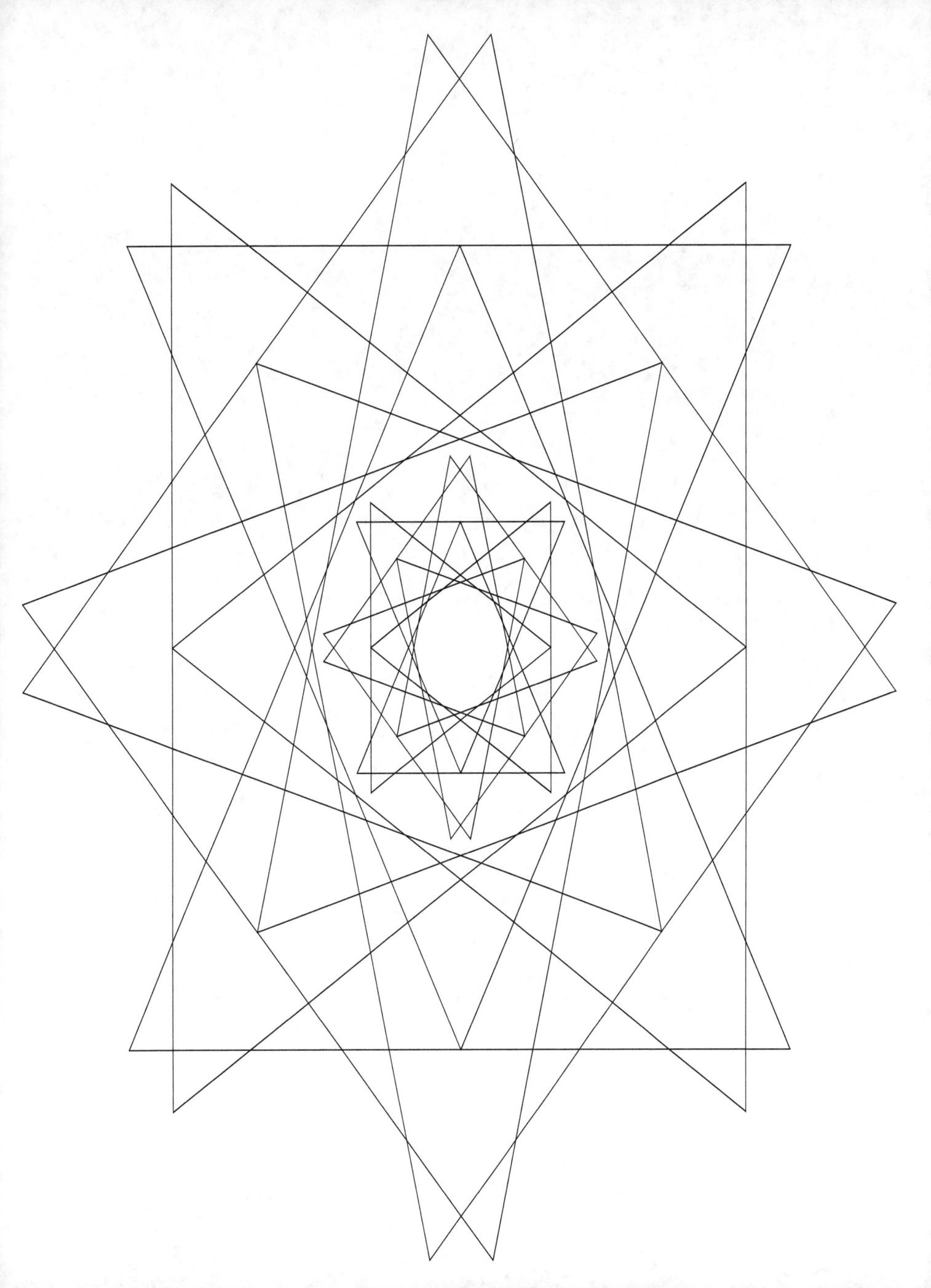

D#   9

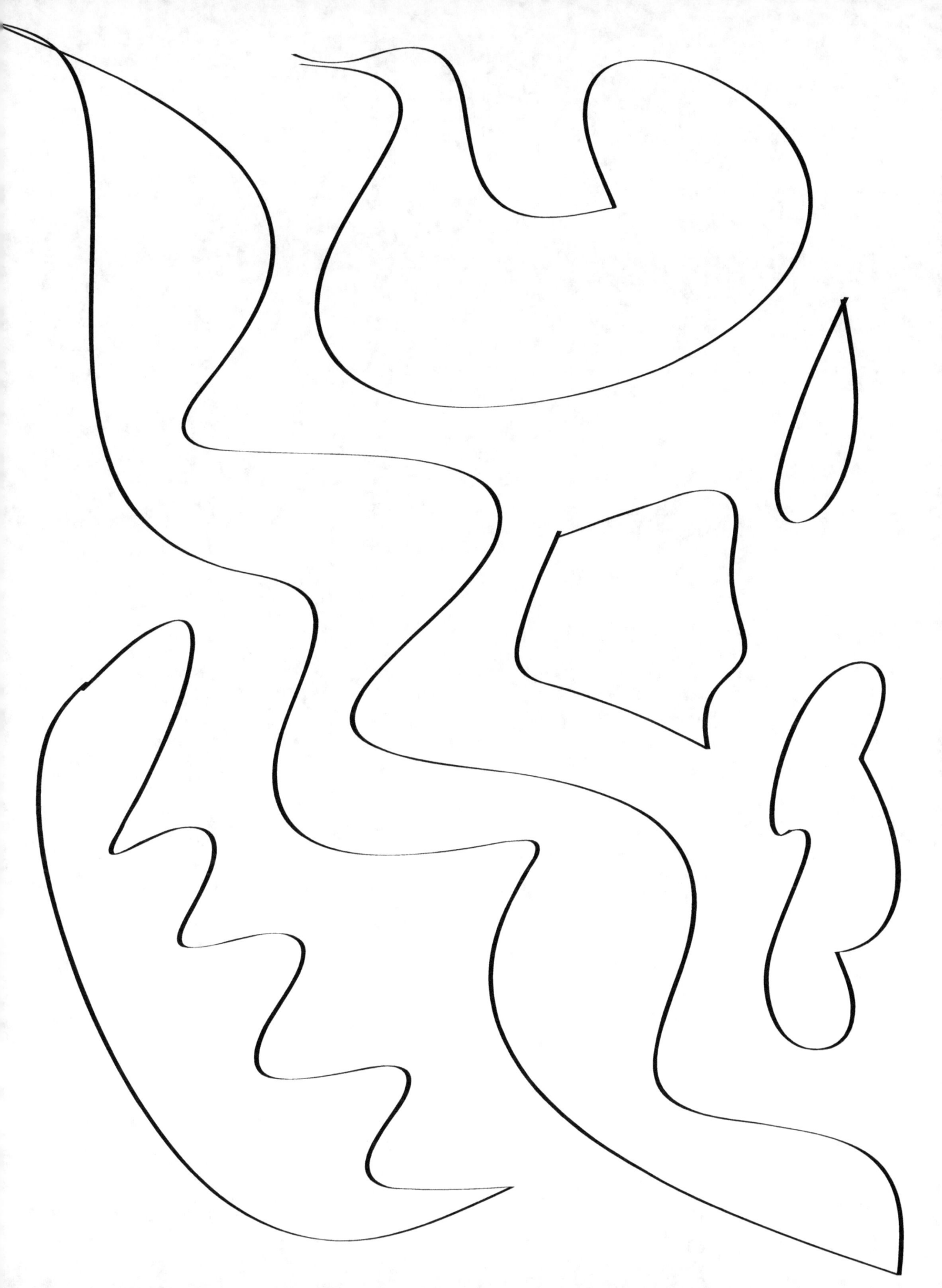

D# 10

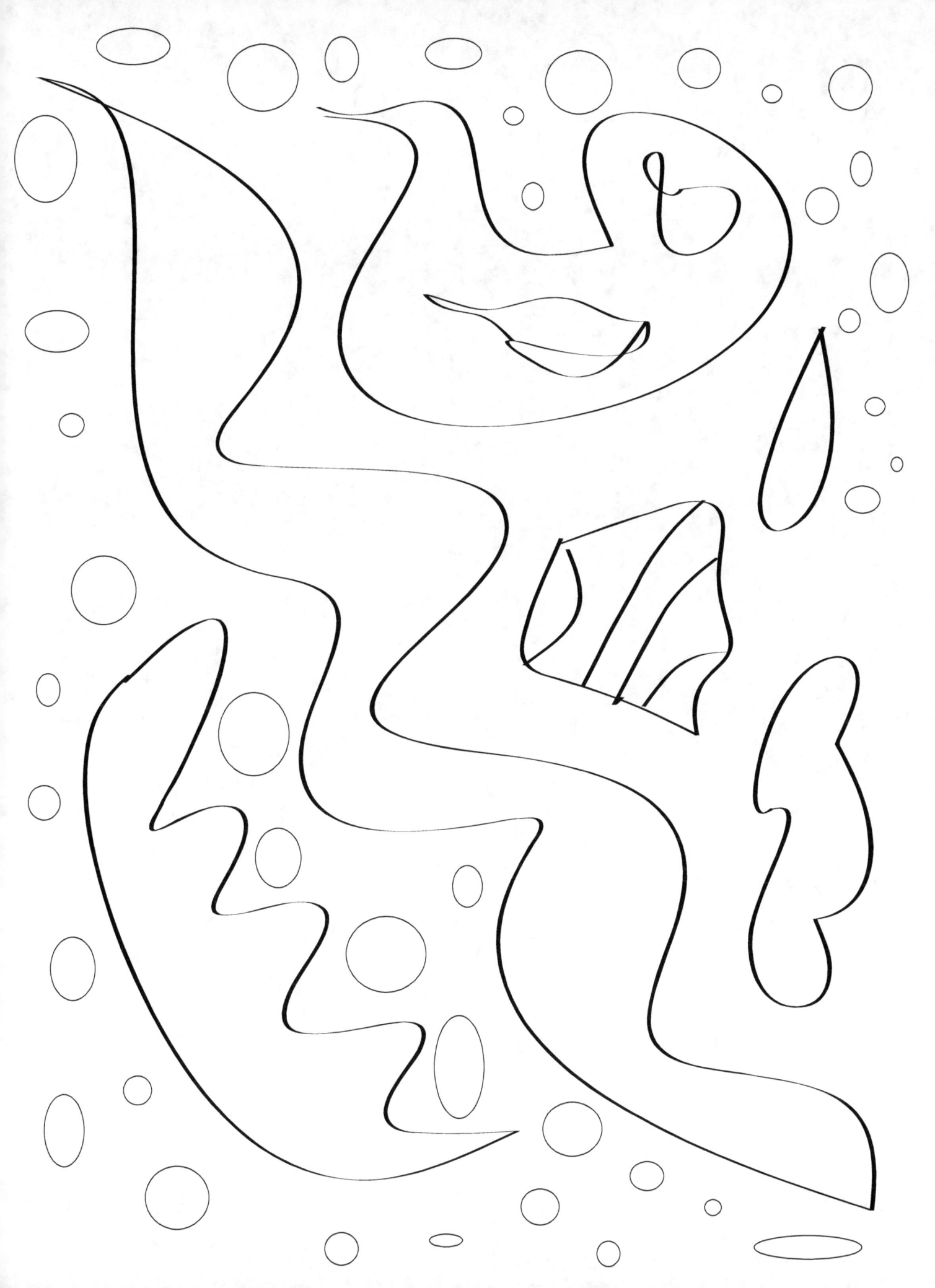

D# 10b

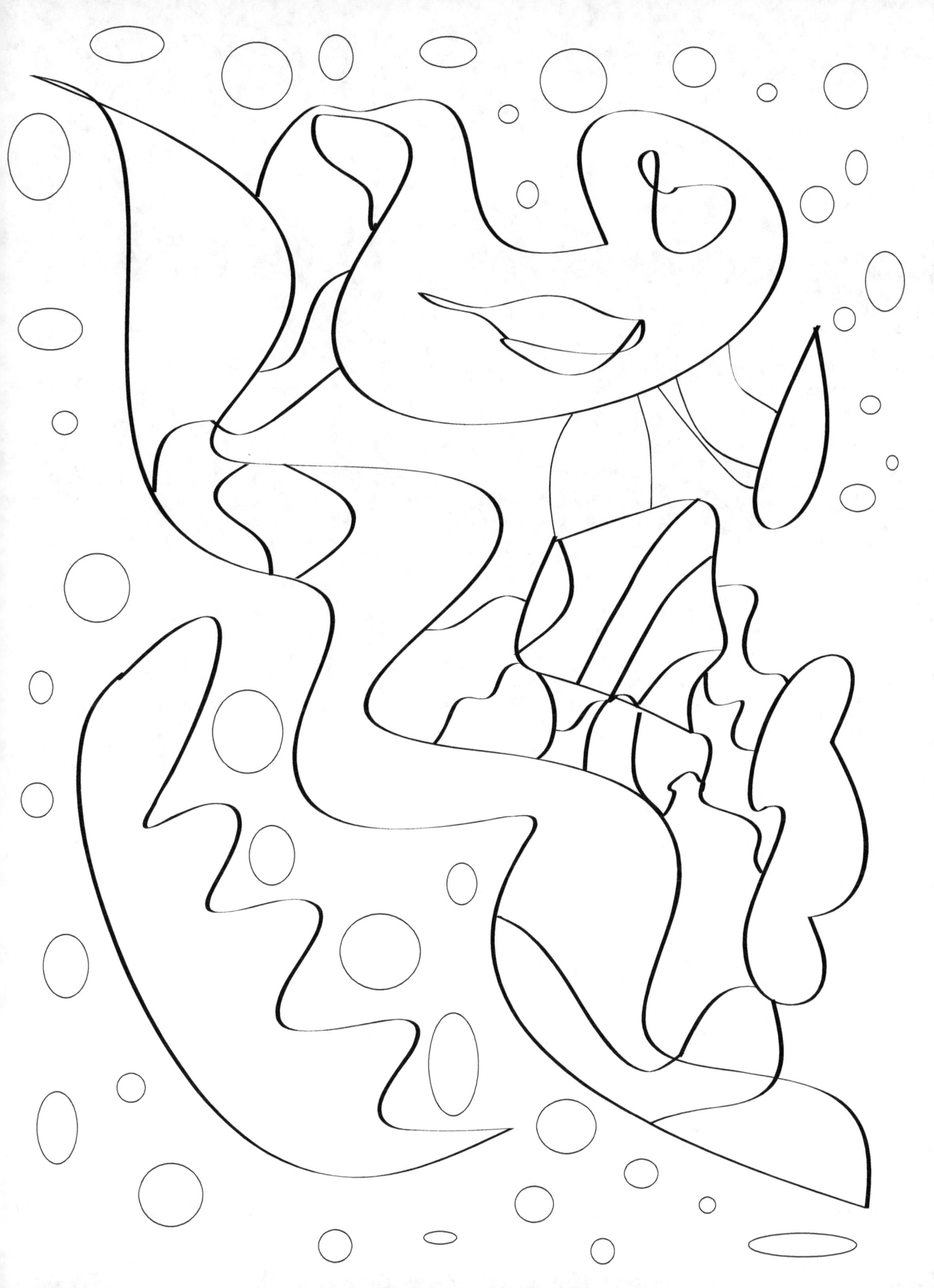

D# 31

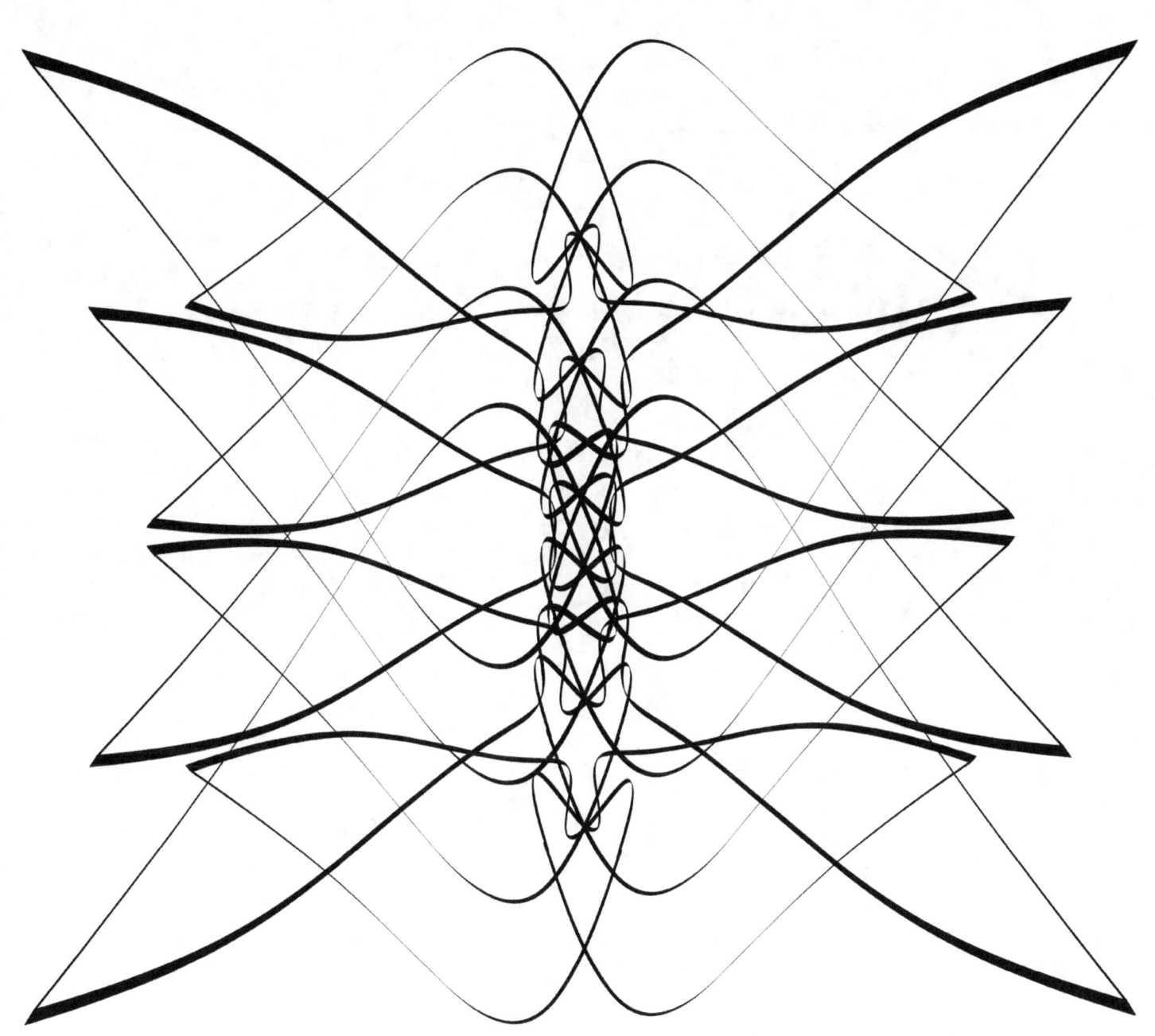

D# 13

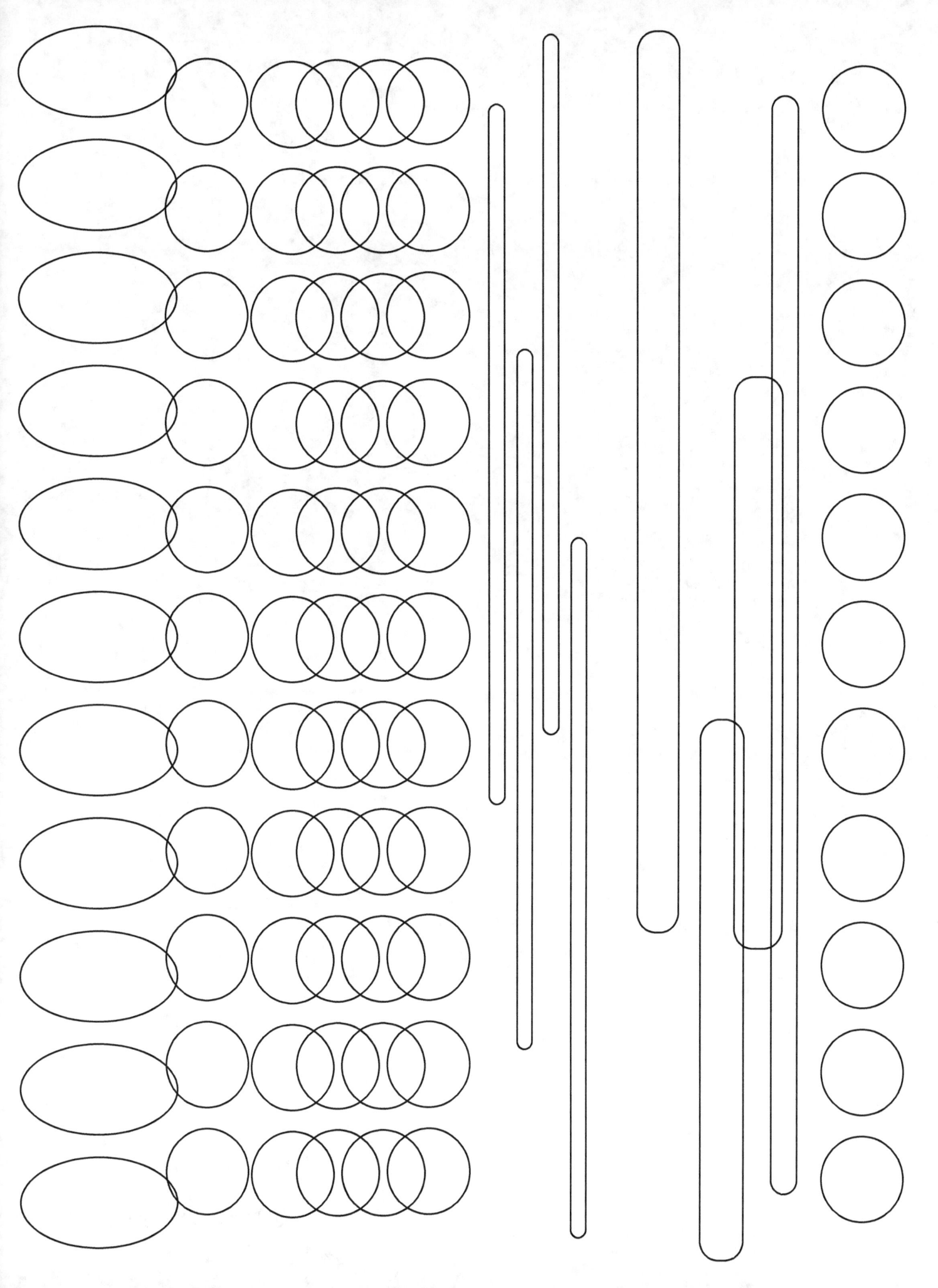

D# 12

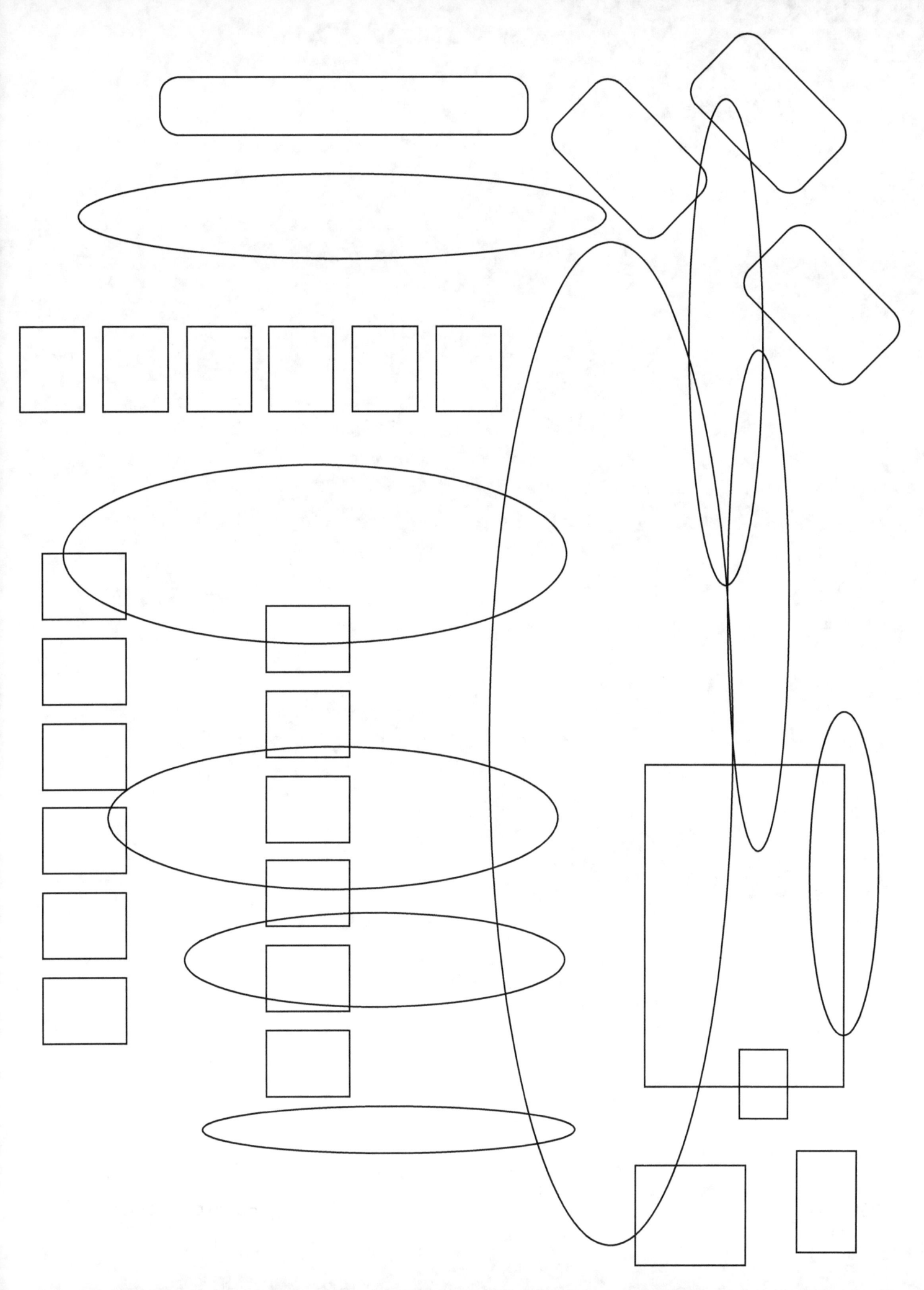

D# 15

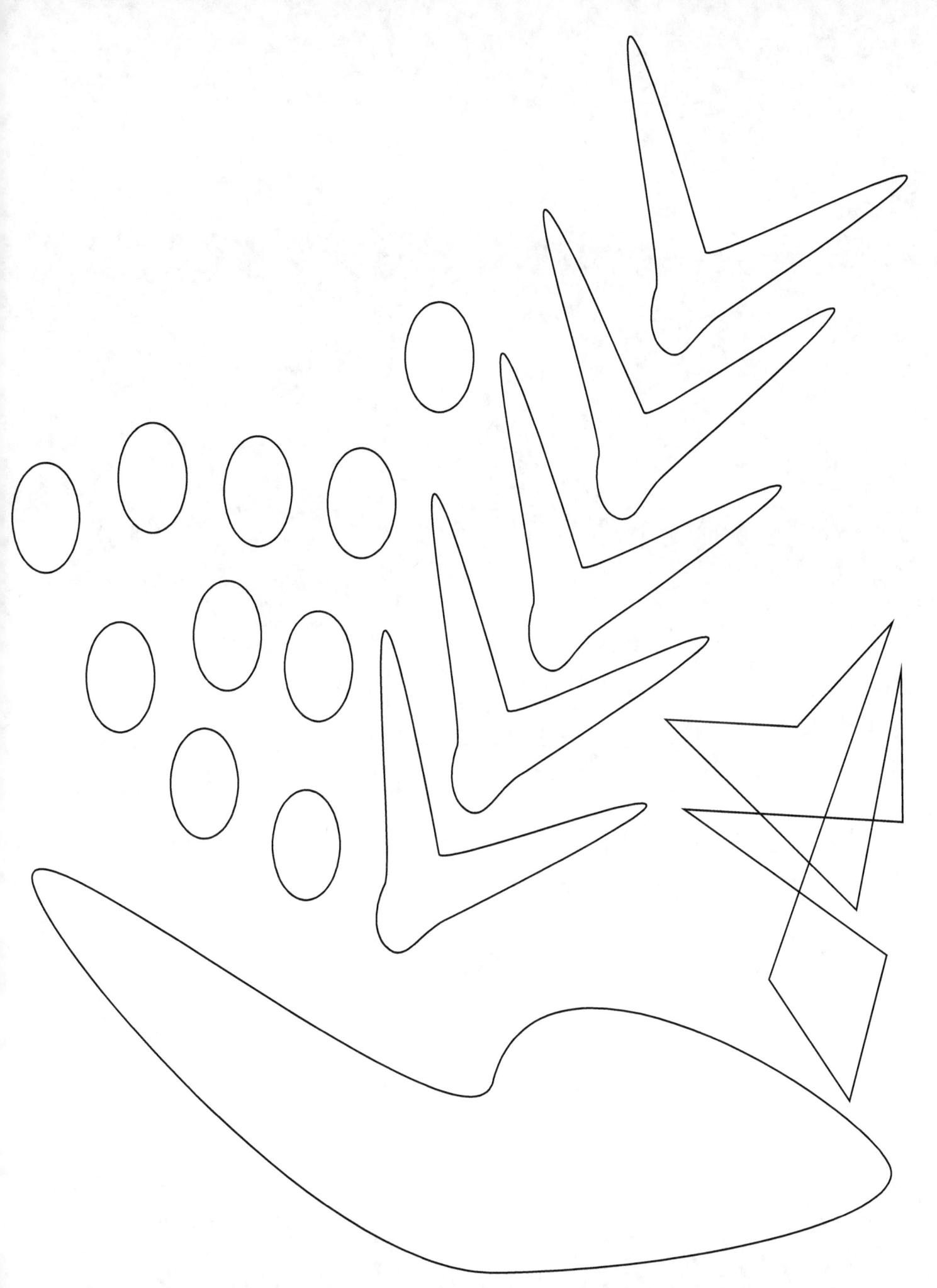

D# 14

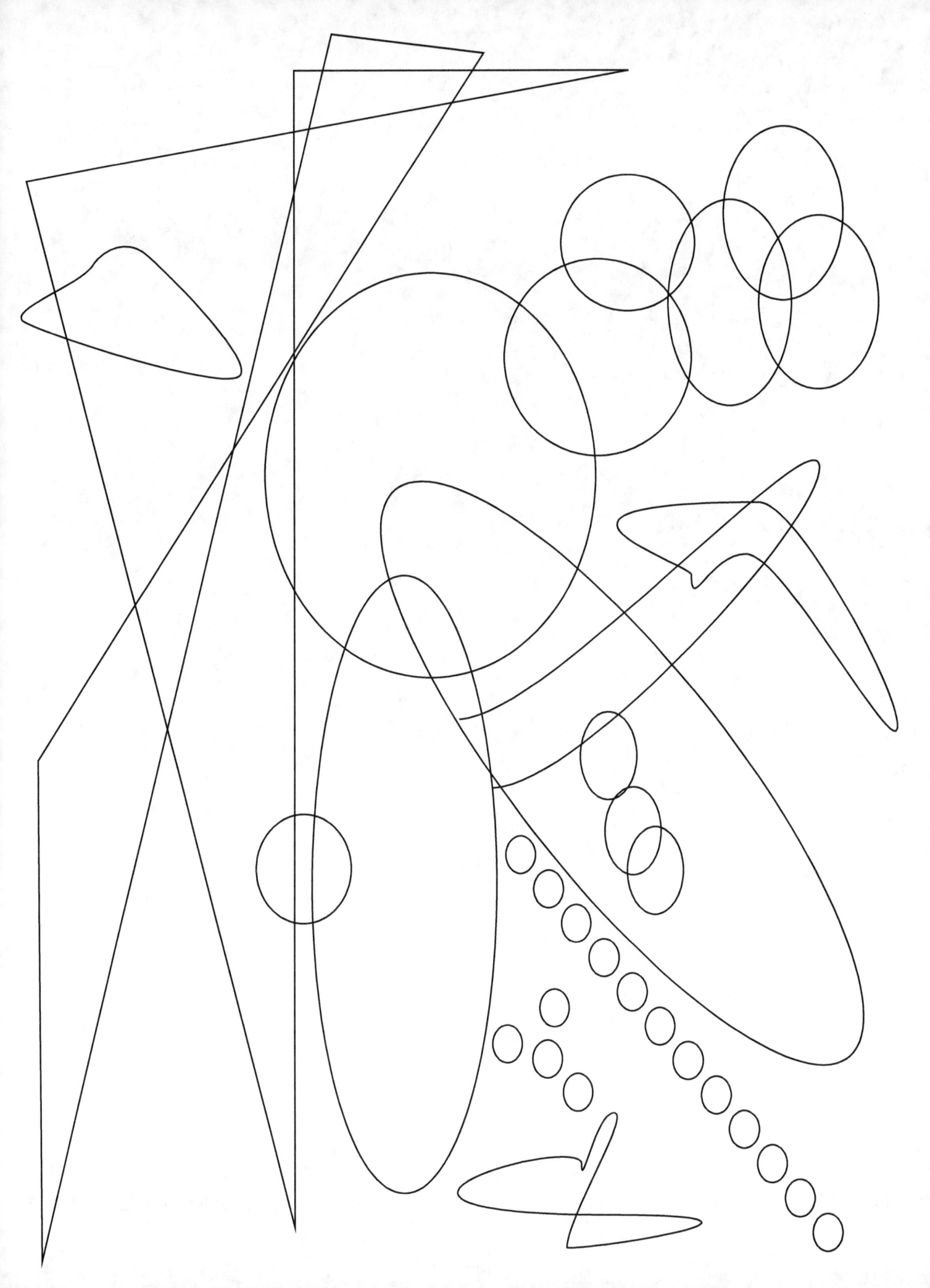

D# 17

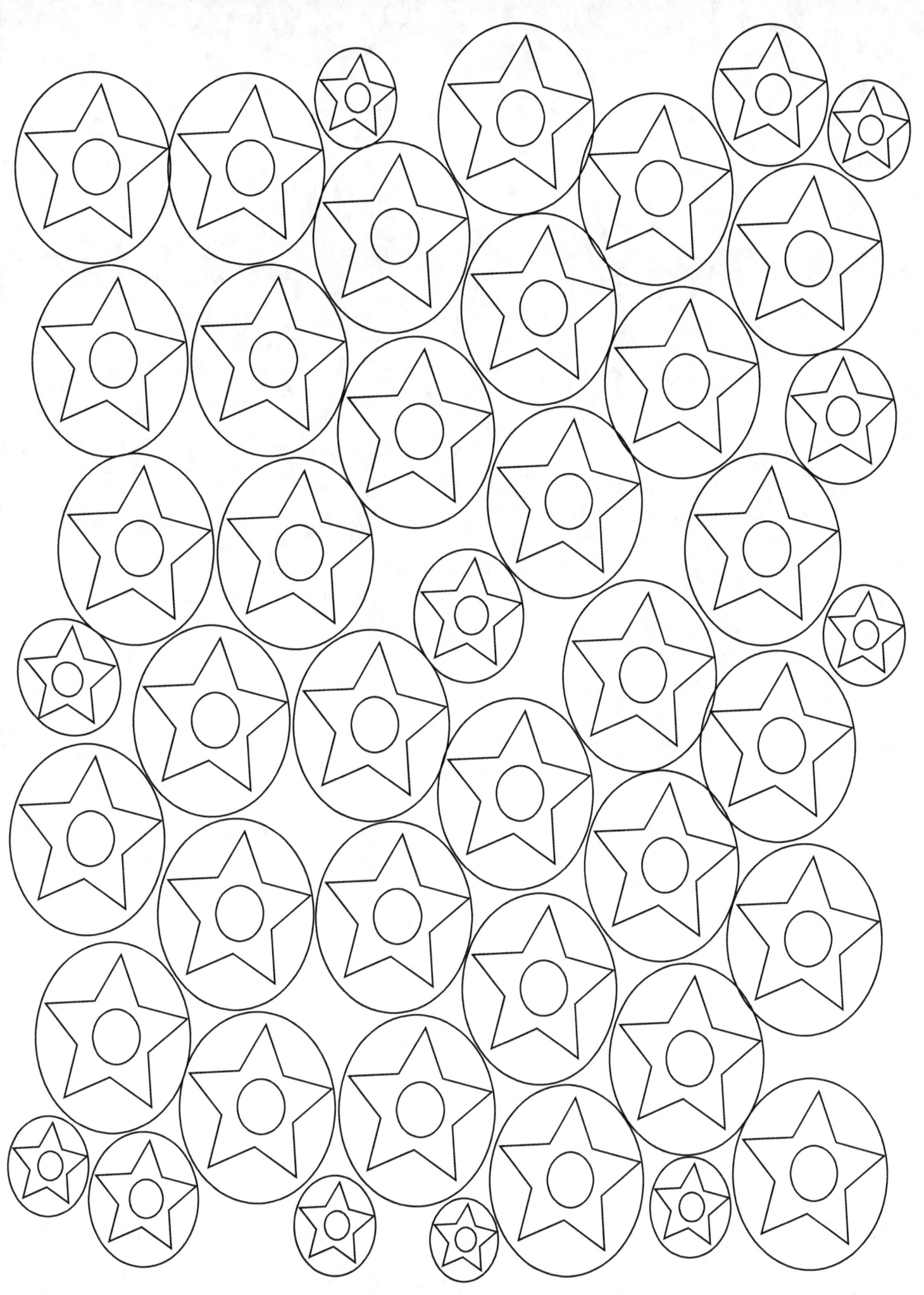

D# 16

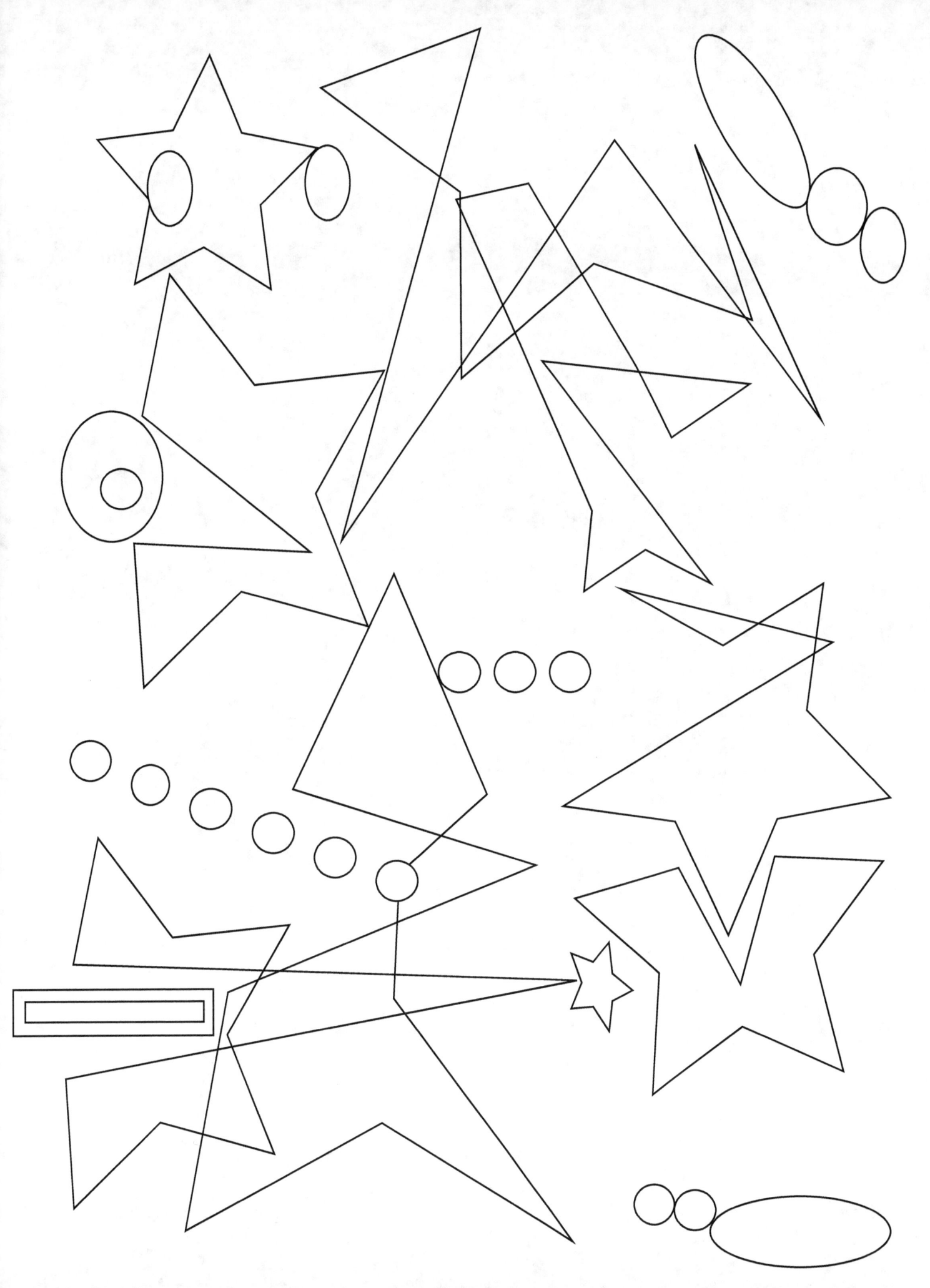

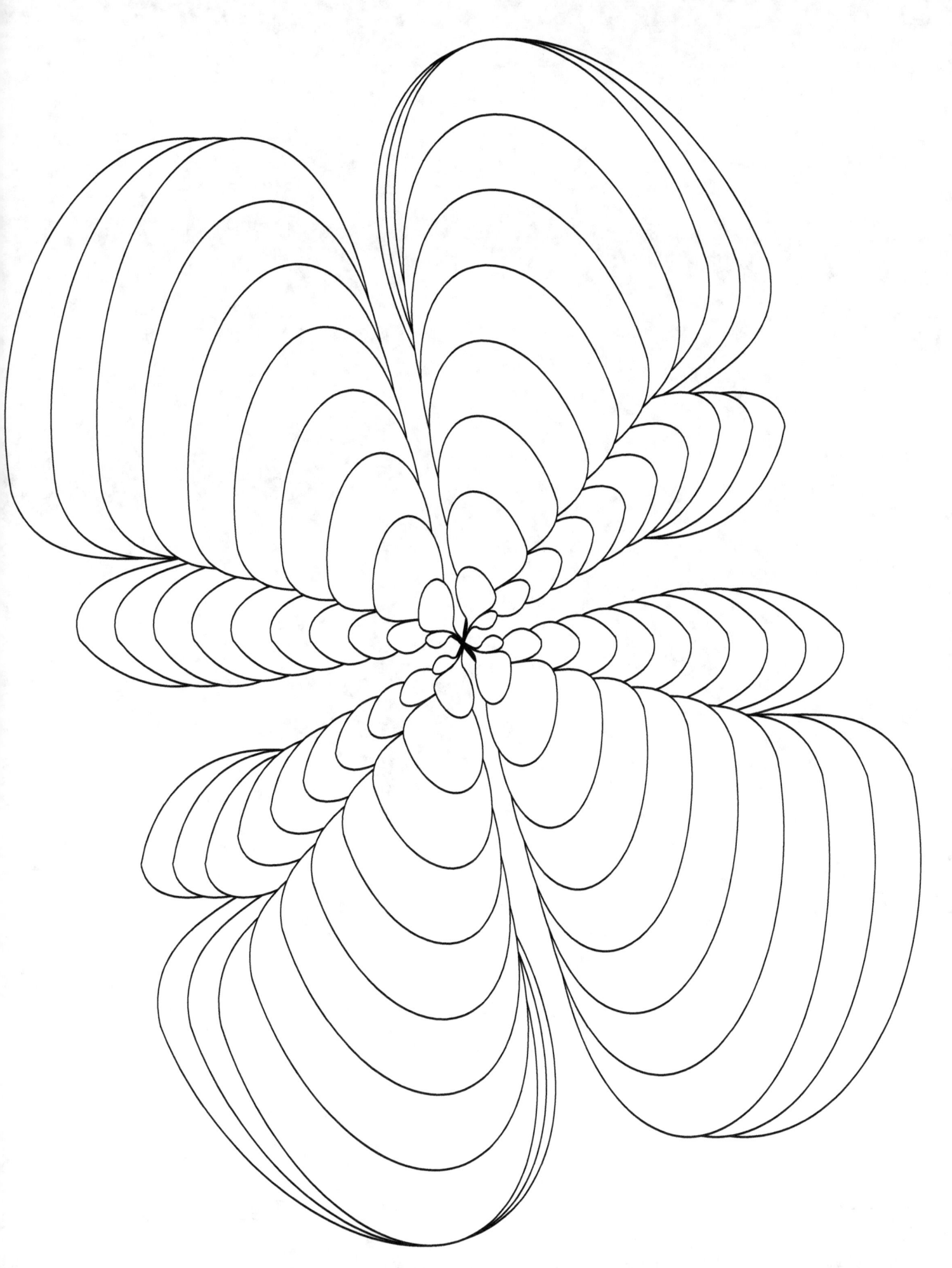

D# 20

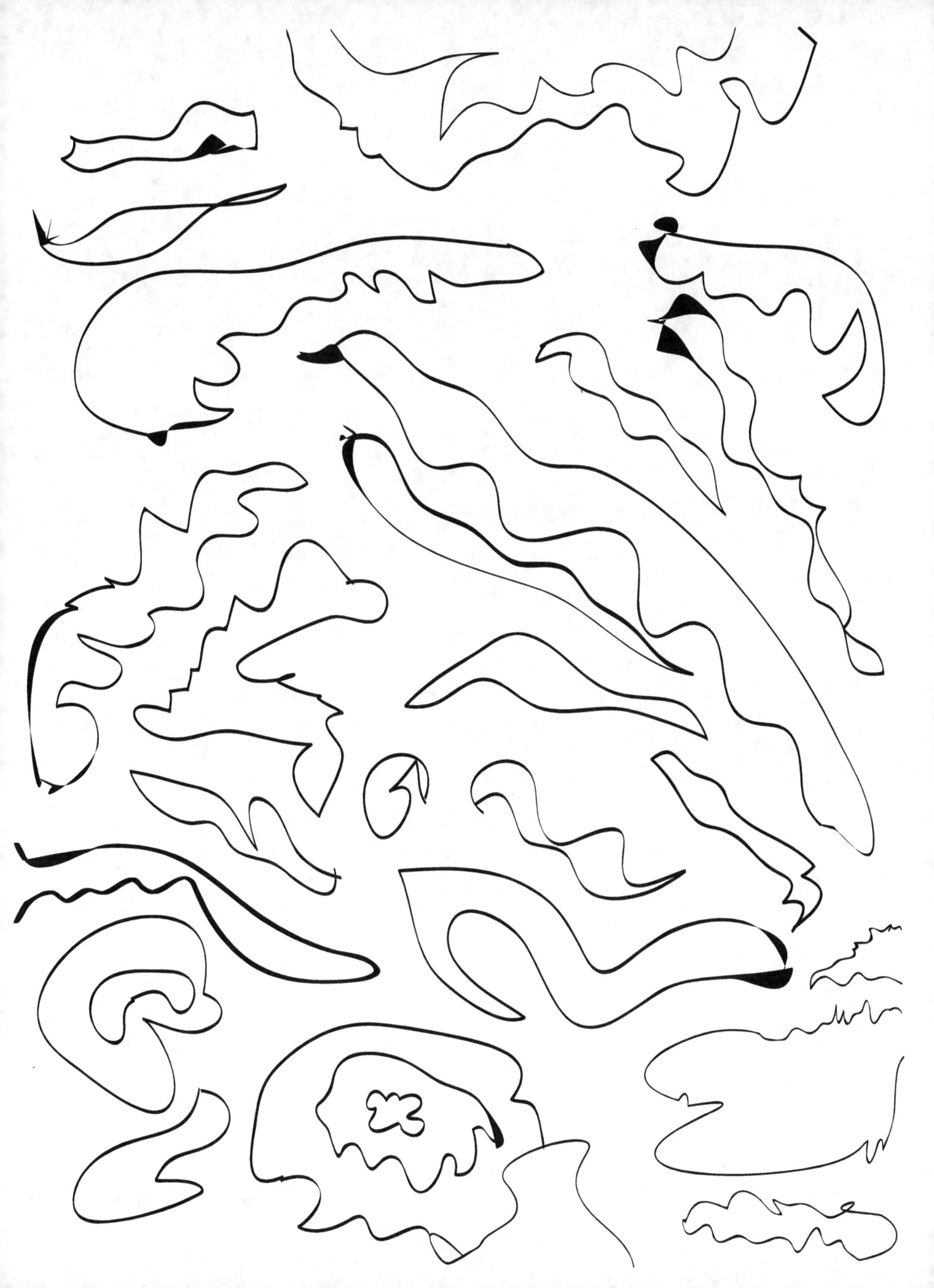

D# 23

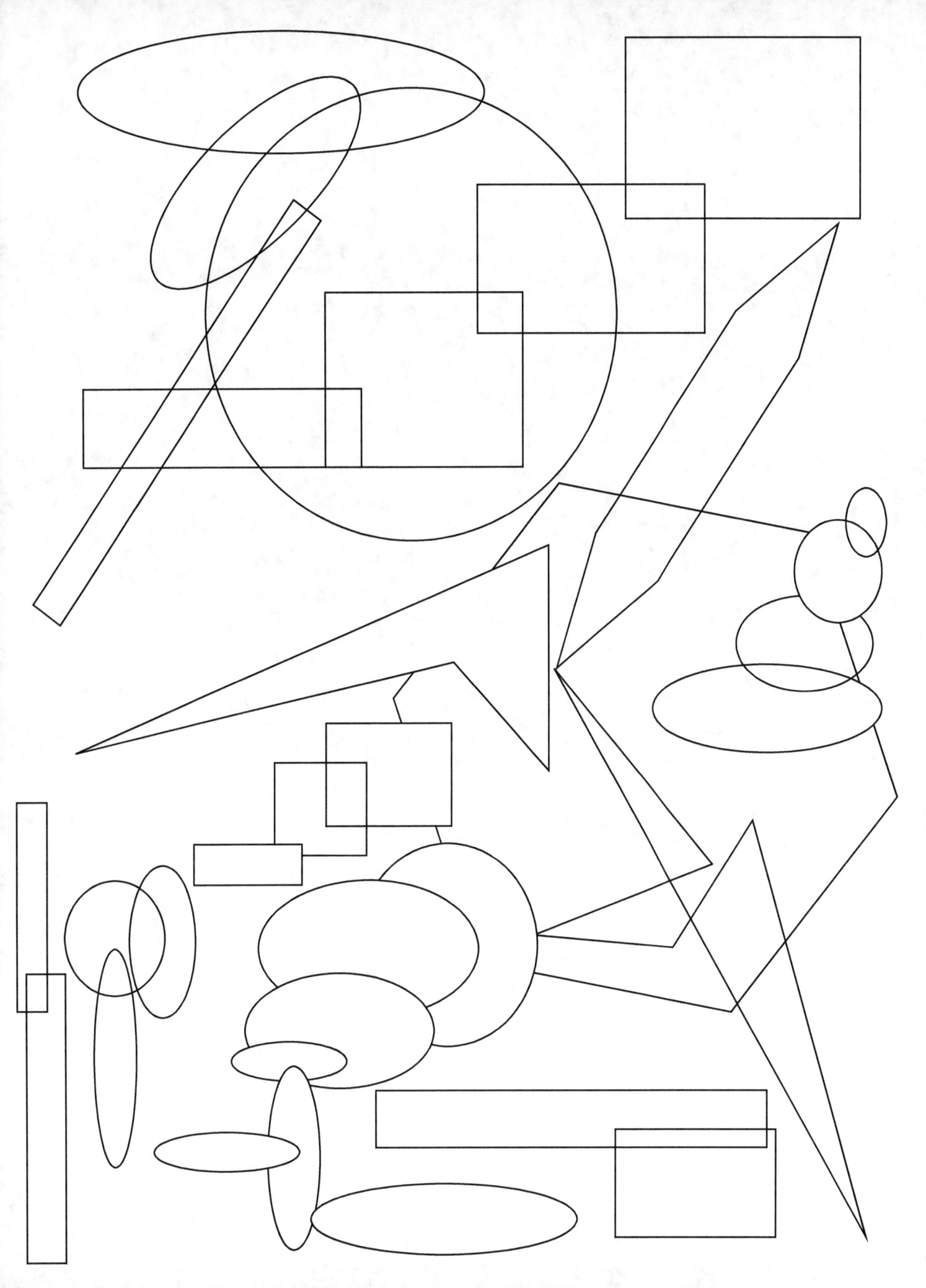

D# 22

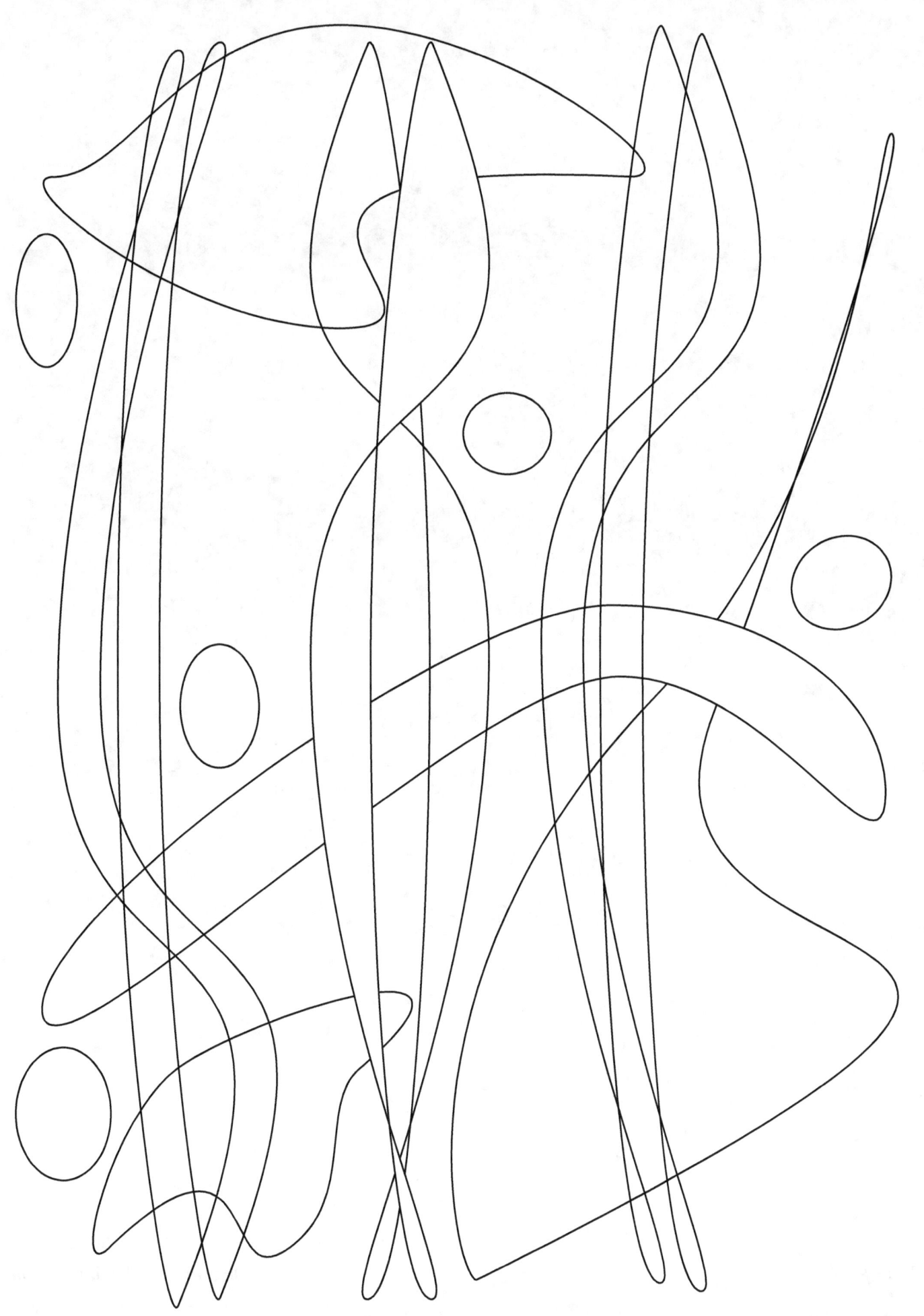

D# 234b

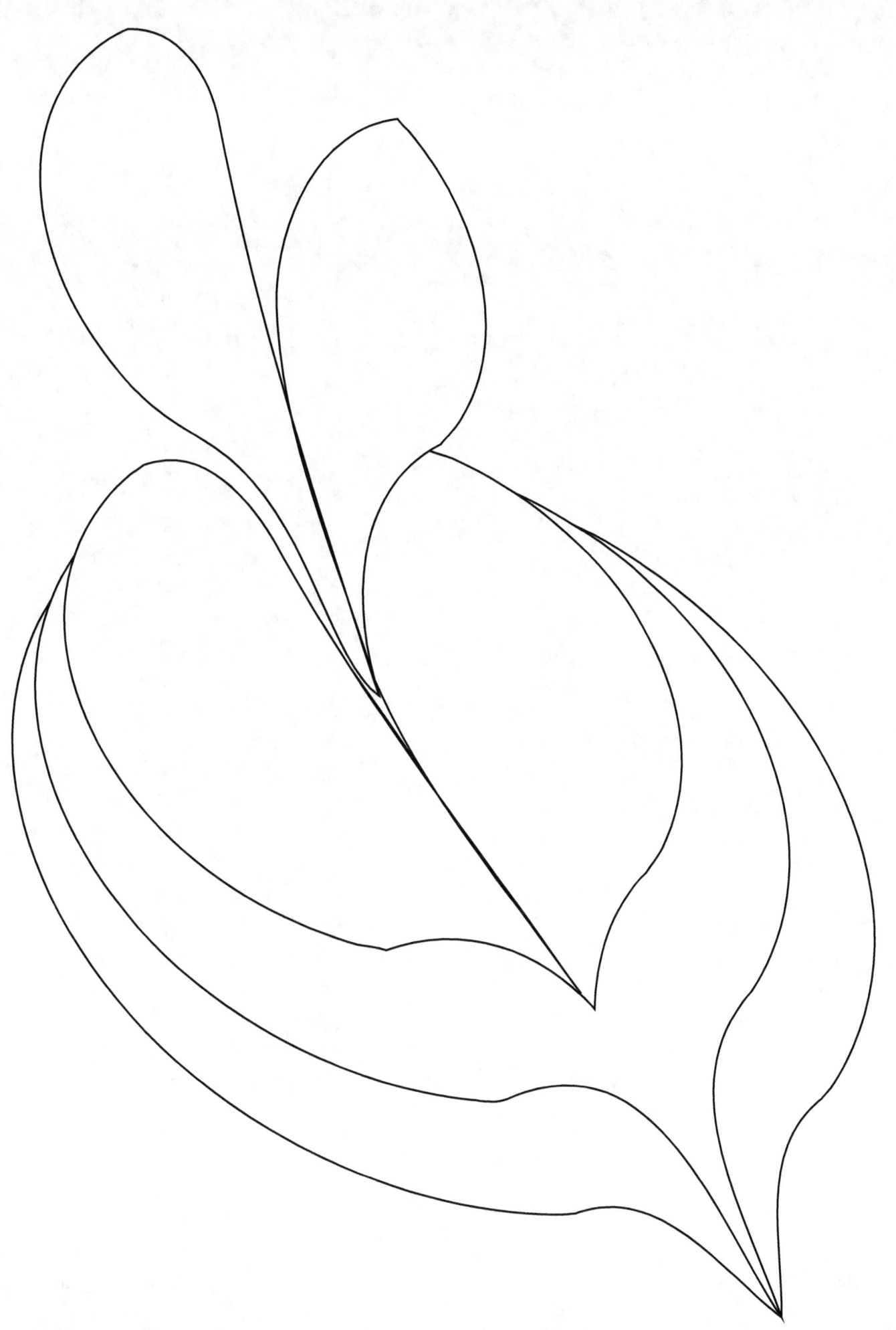

D# 24

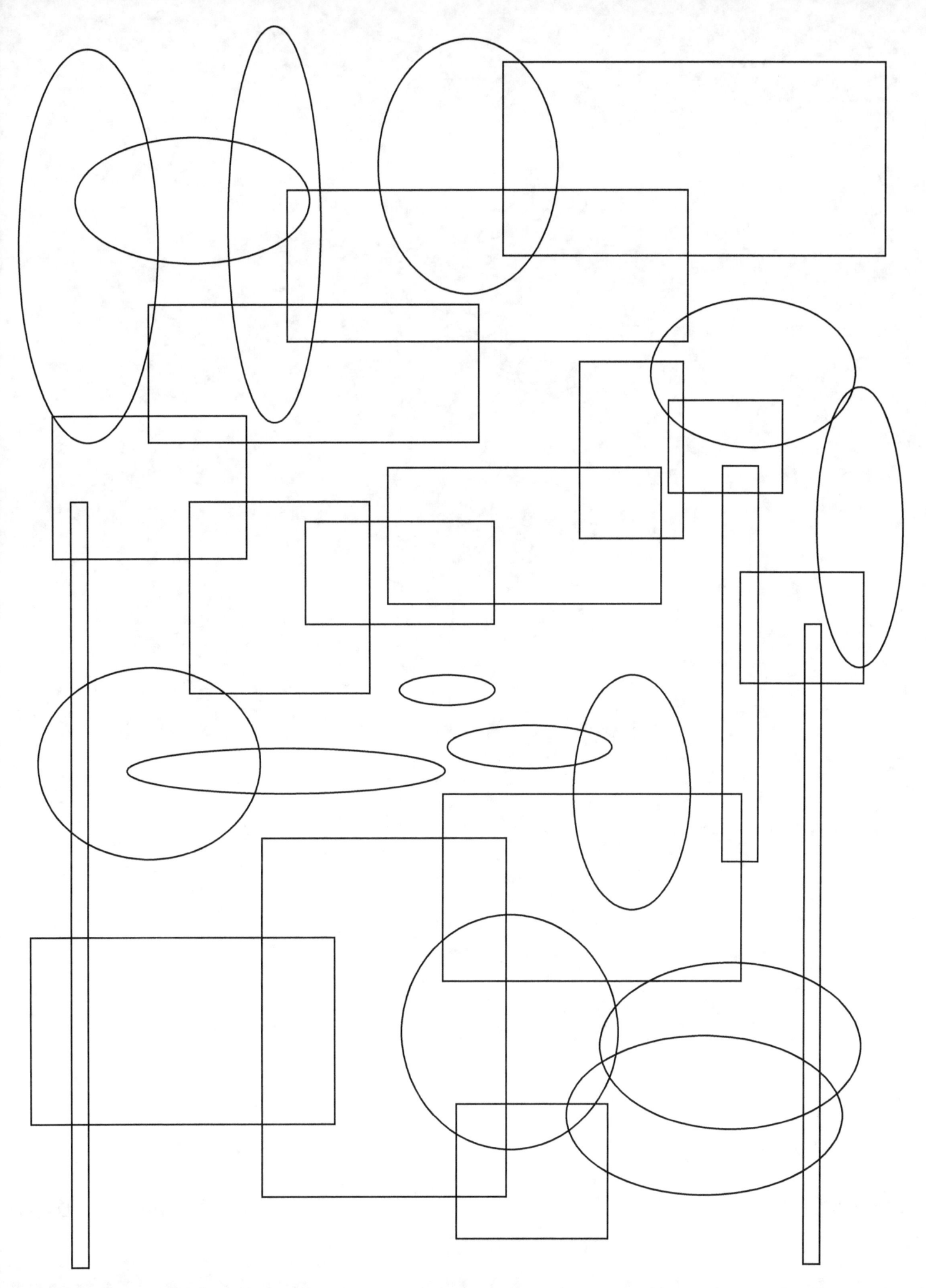

D# 27b

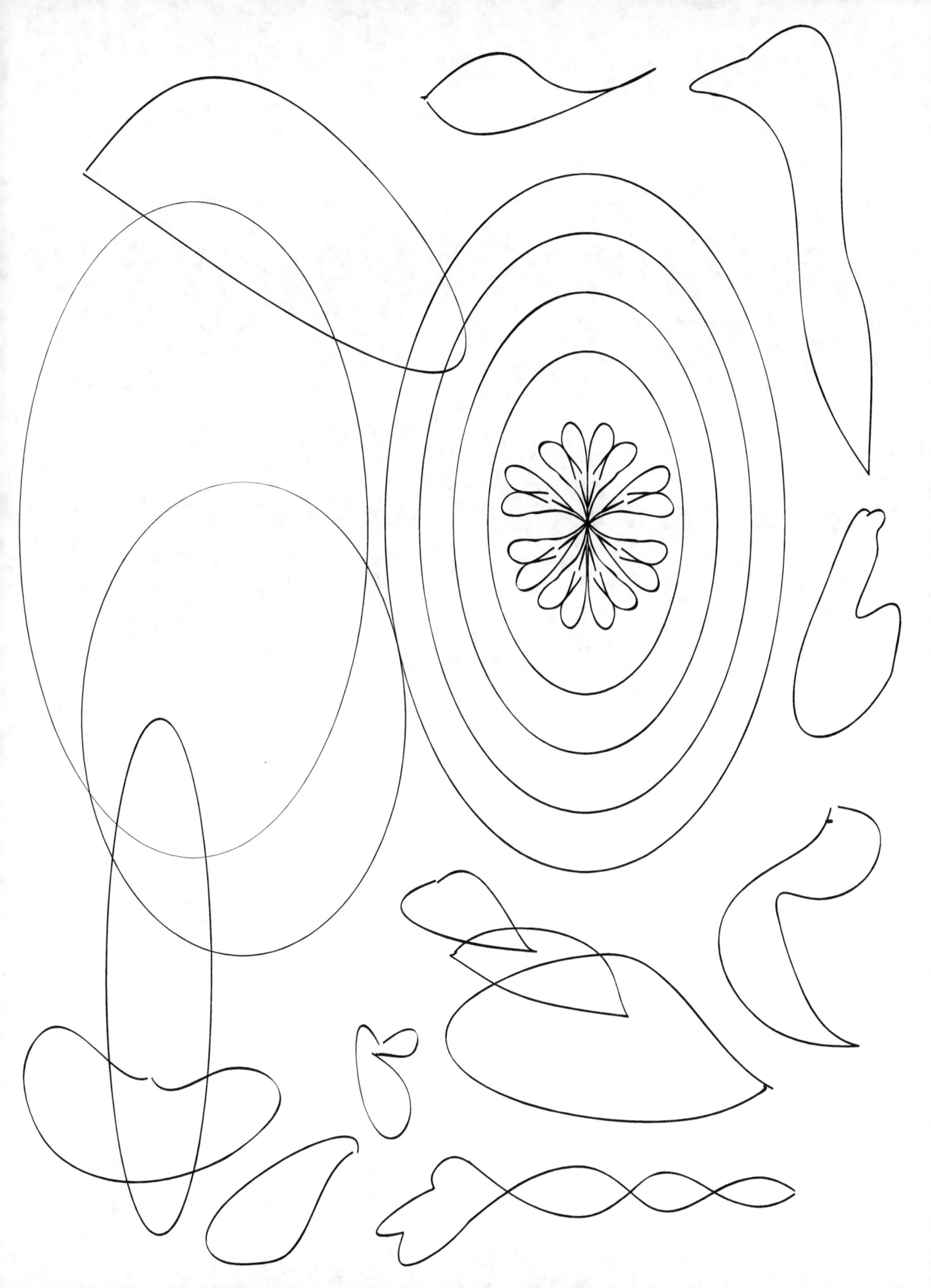

D# 26b

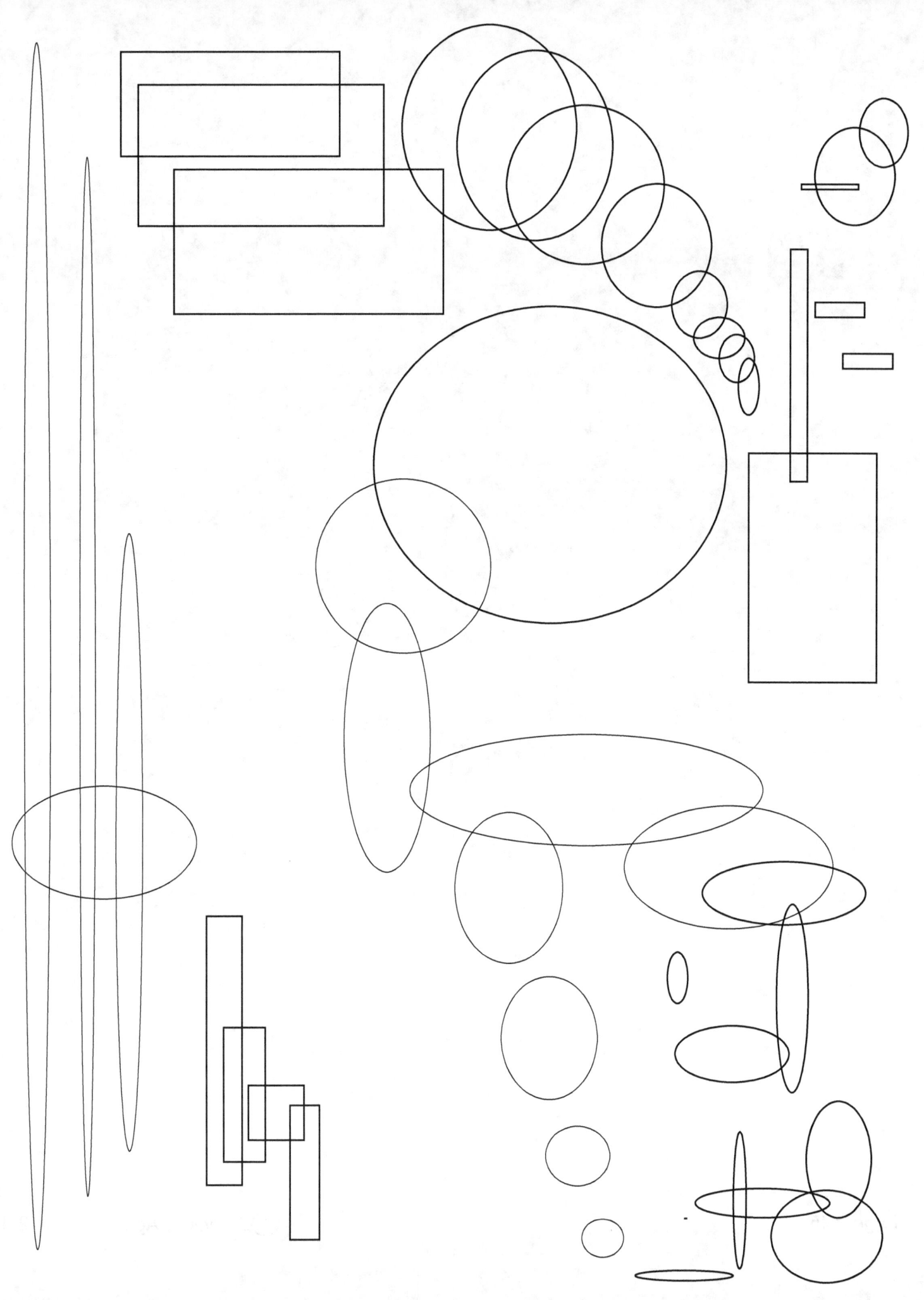

D# 269

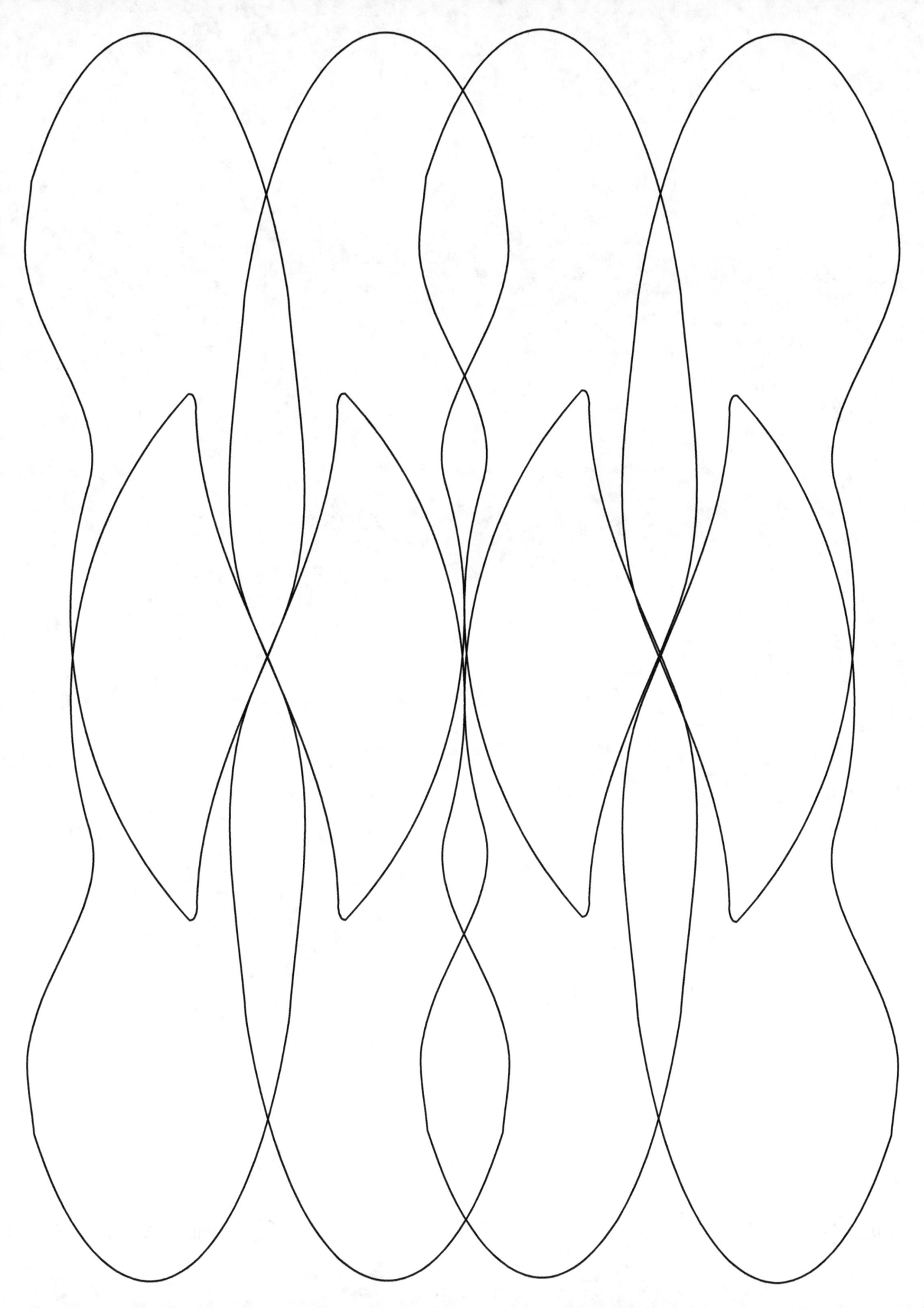

D# 232

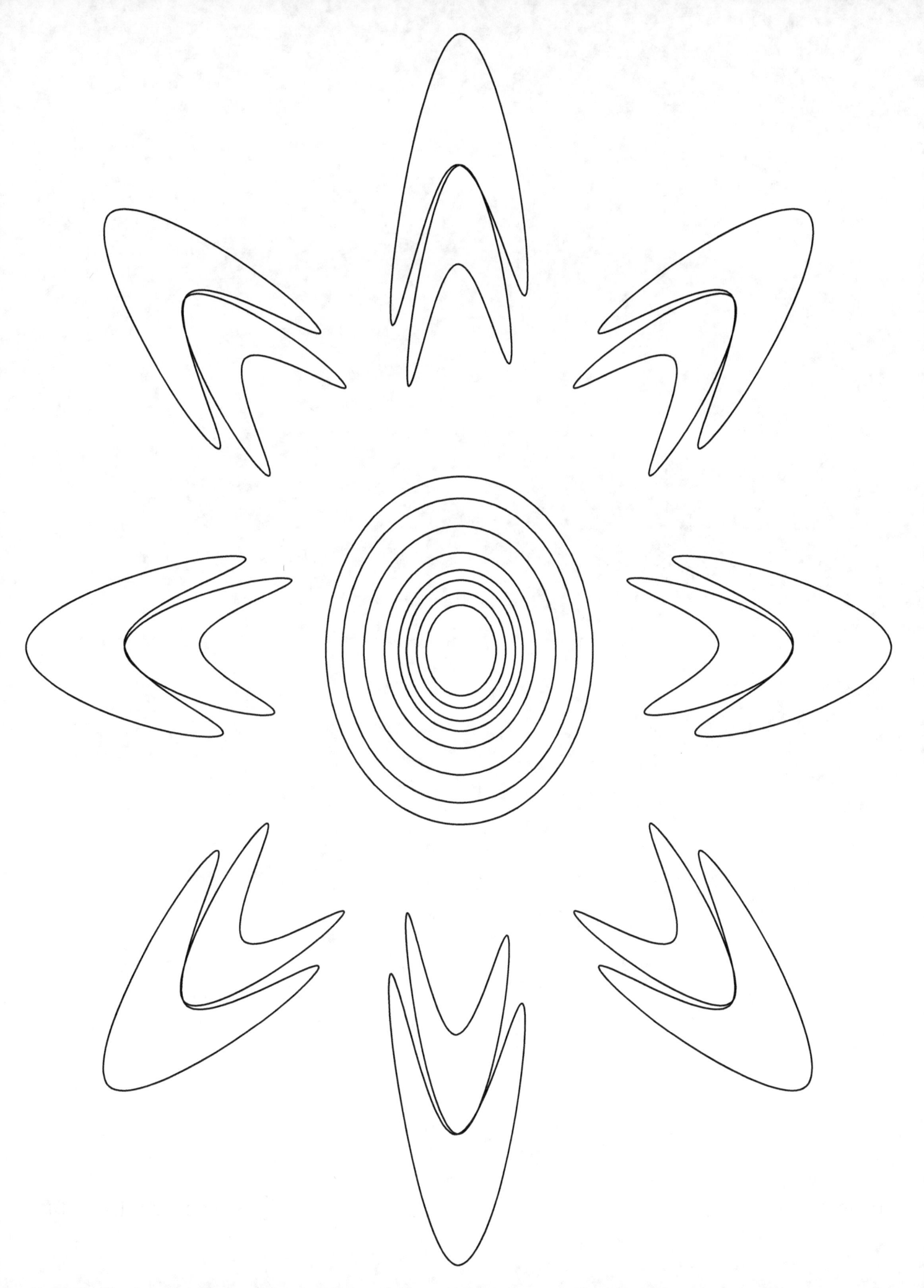

D# 30

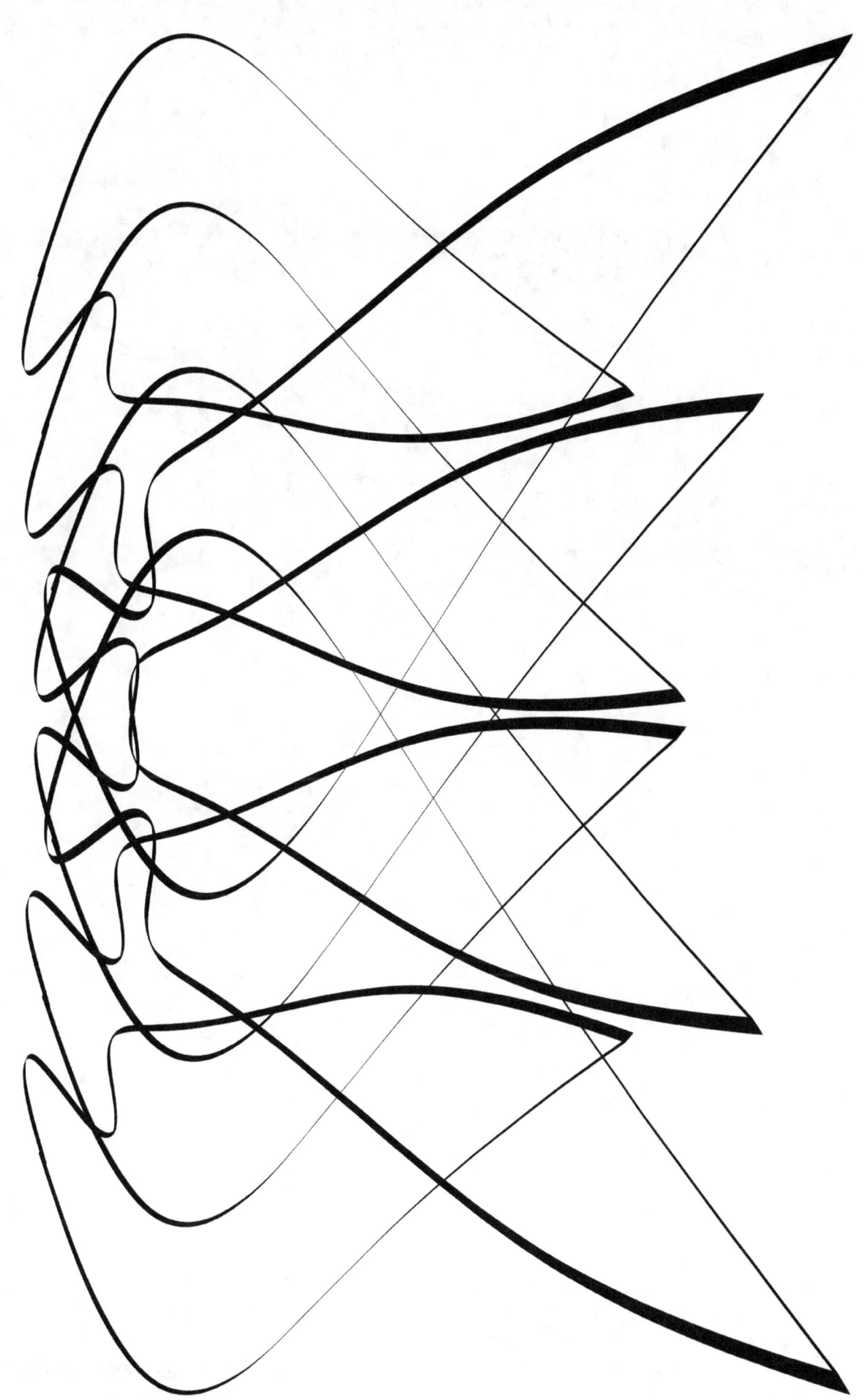

D# 29

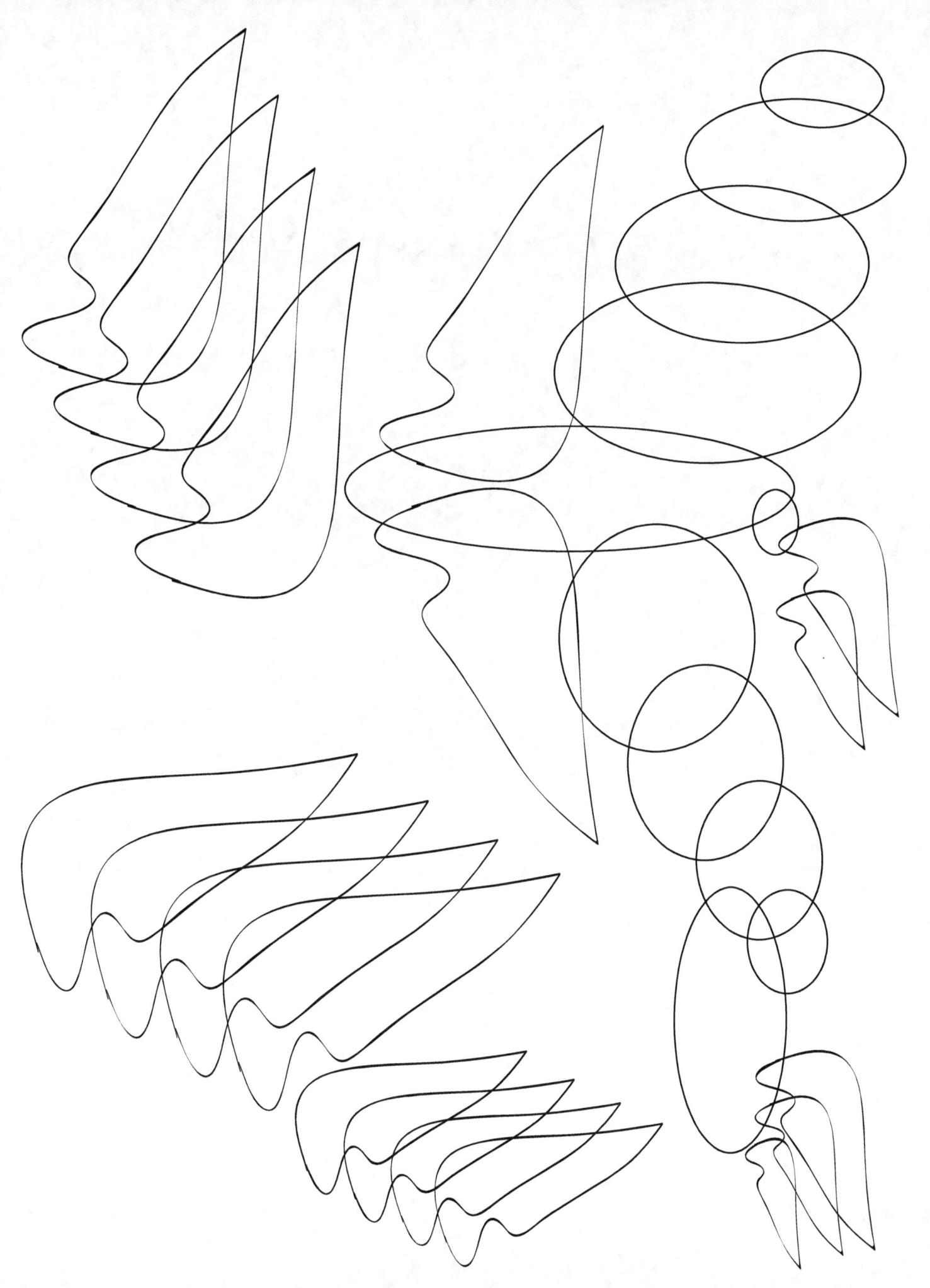

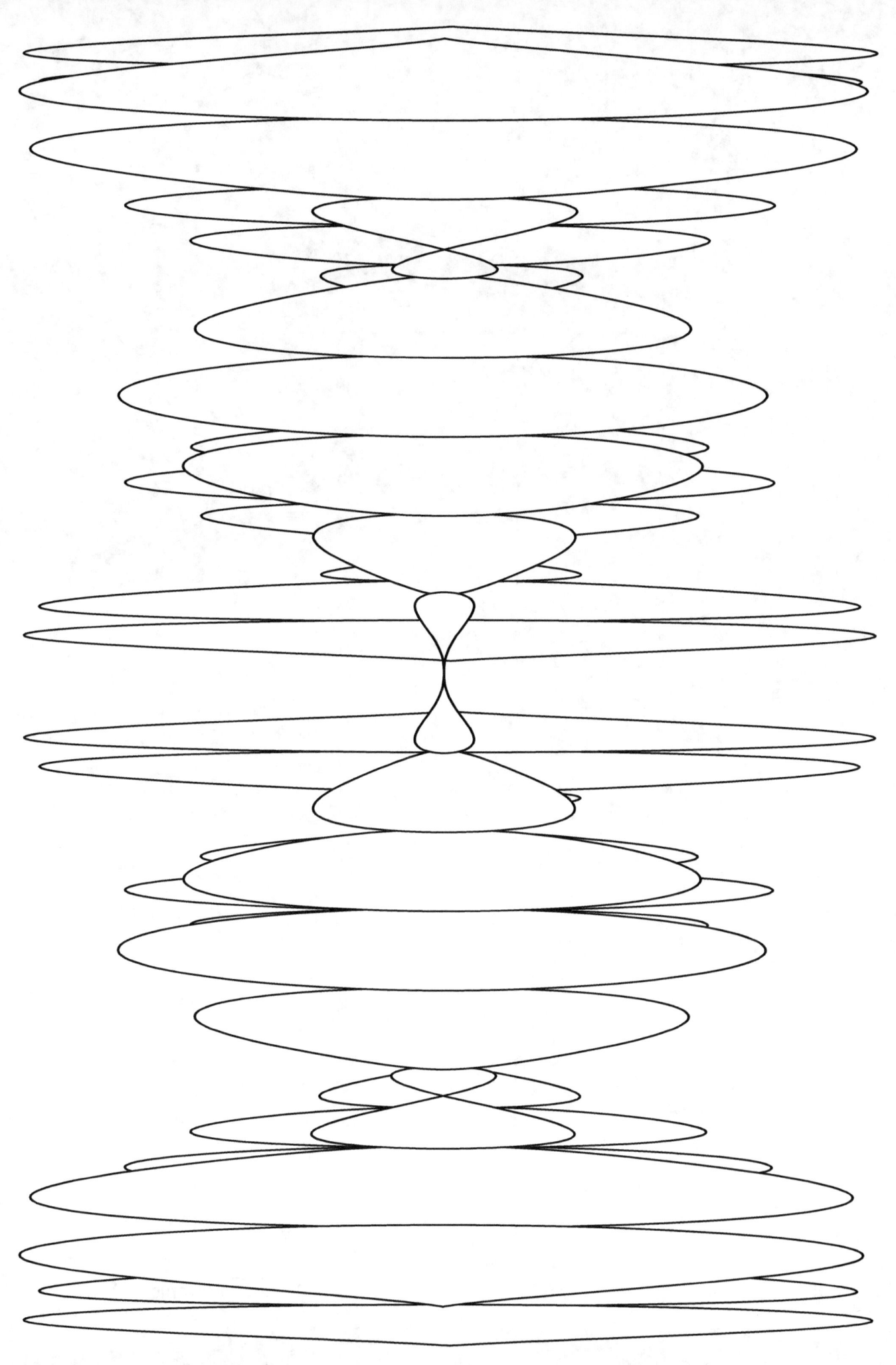

D#   6

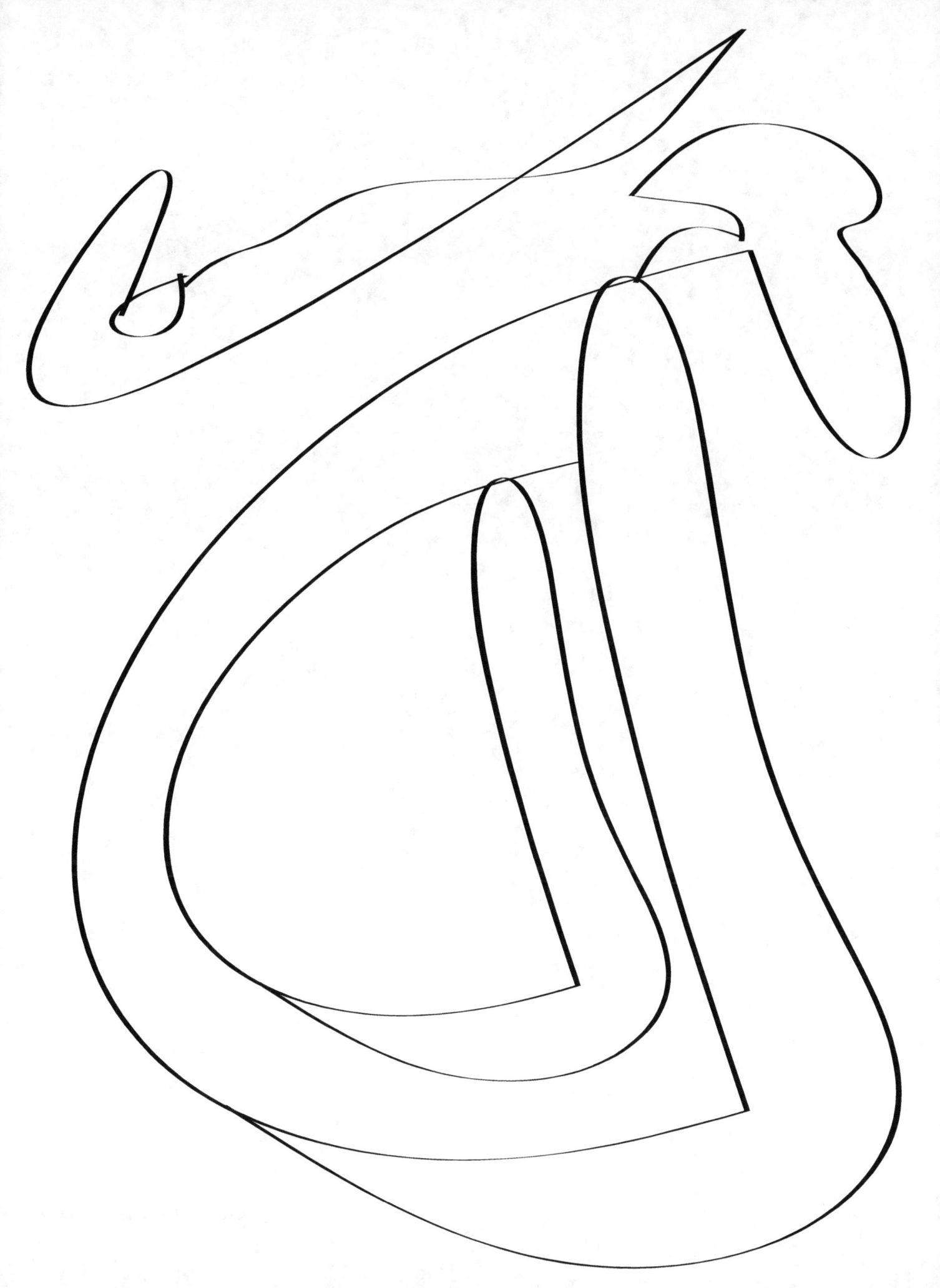

D# 34

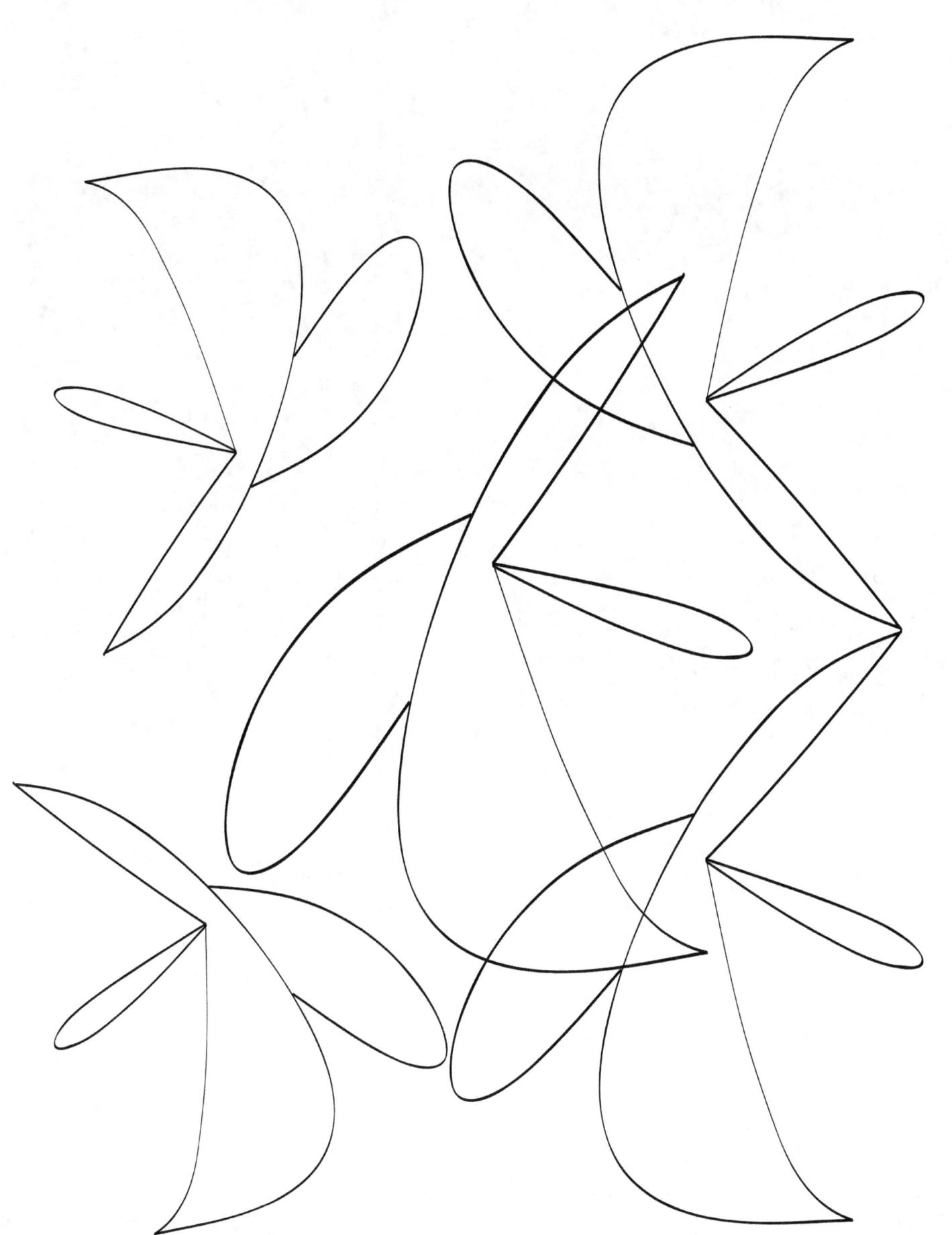

D# 33

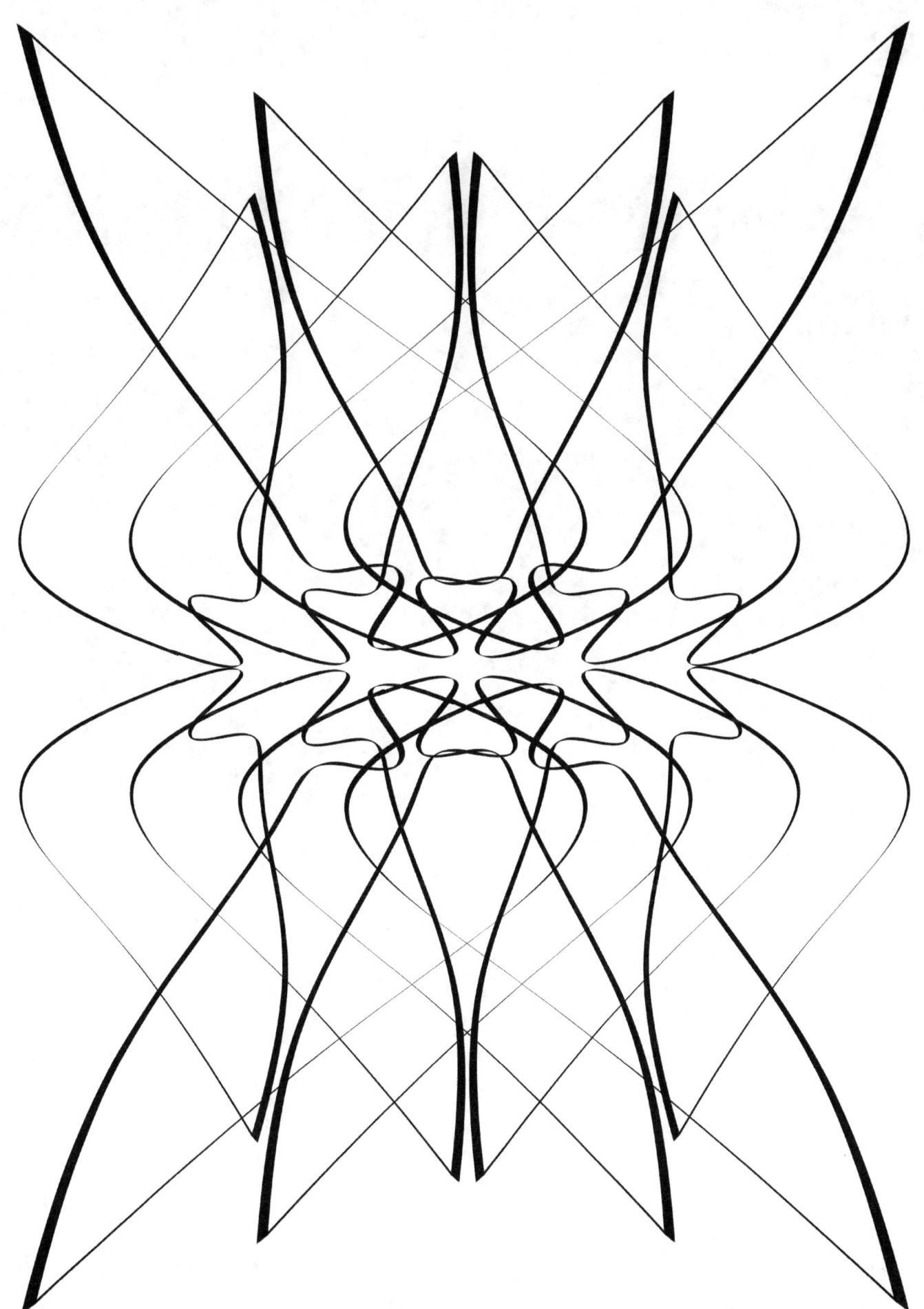

D# 36

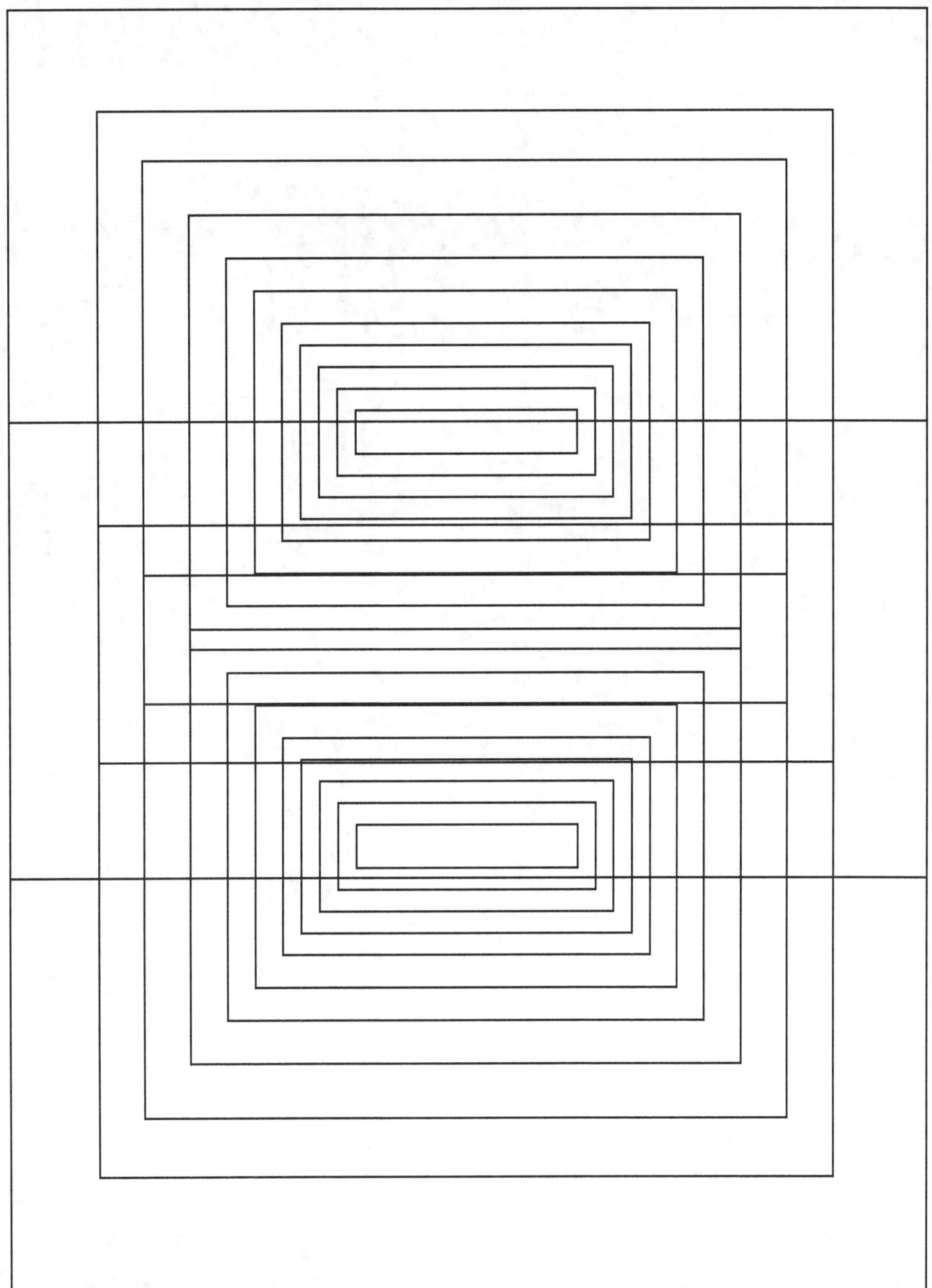

D# 35

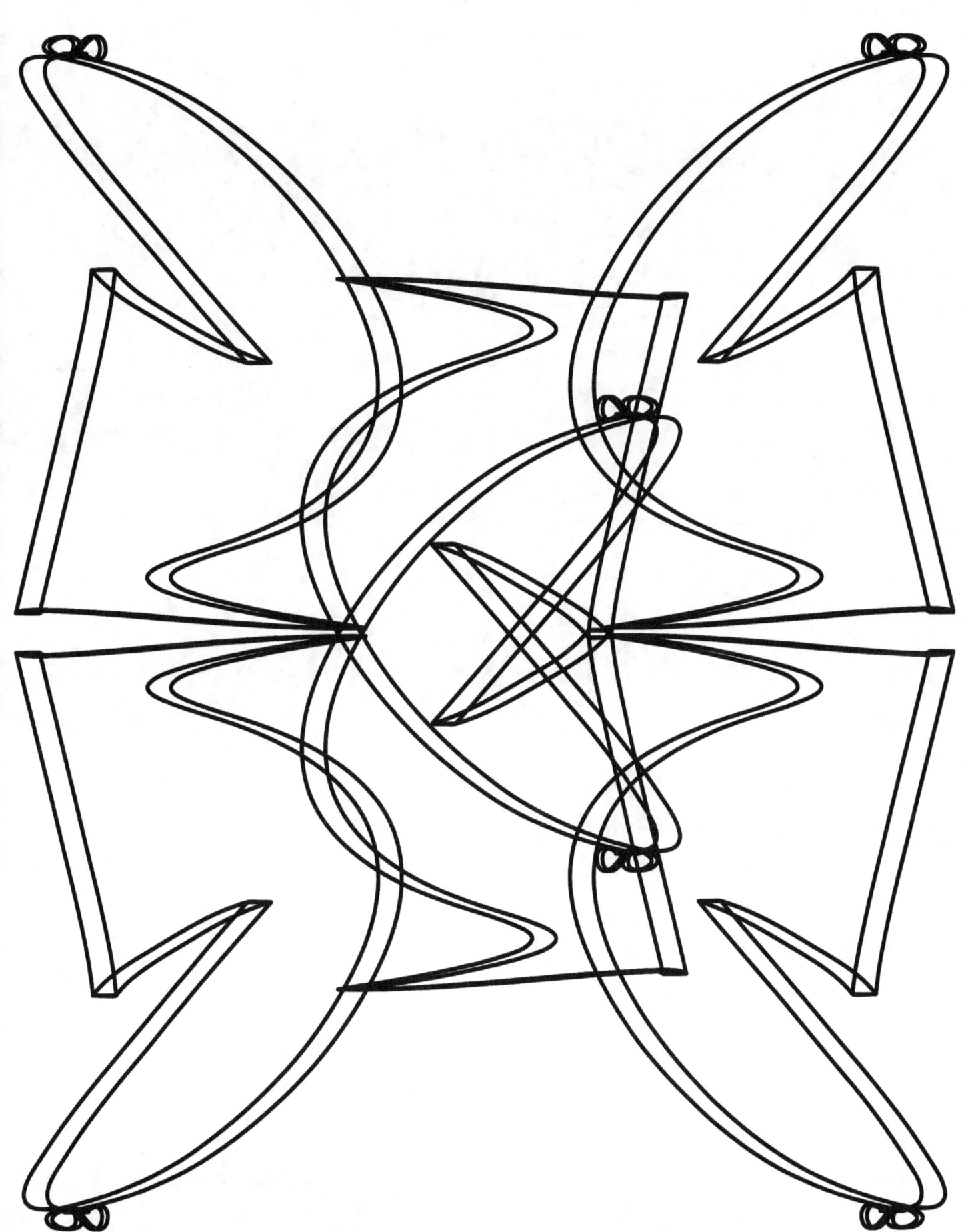

D# 38

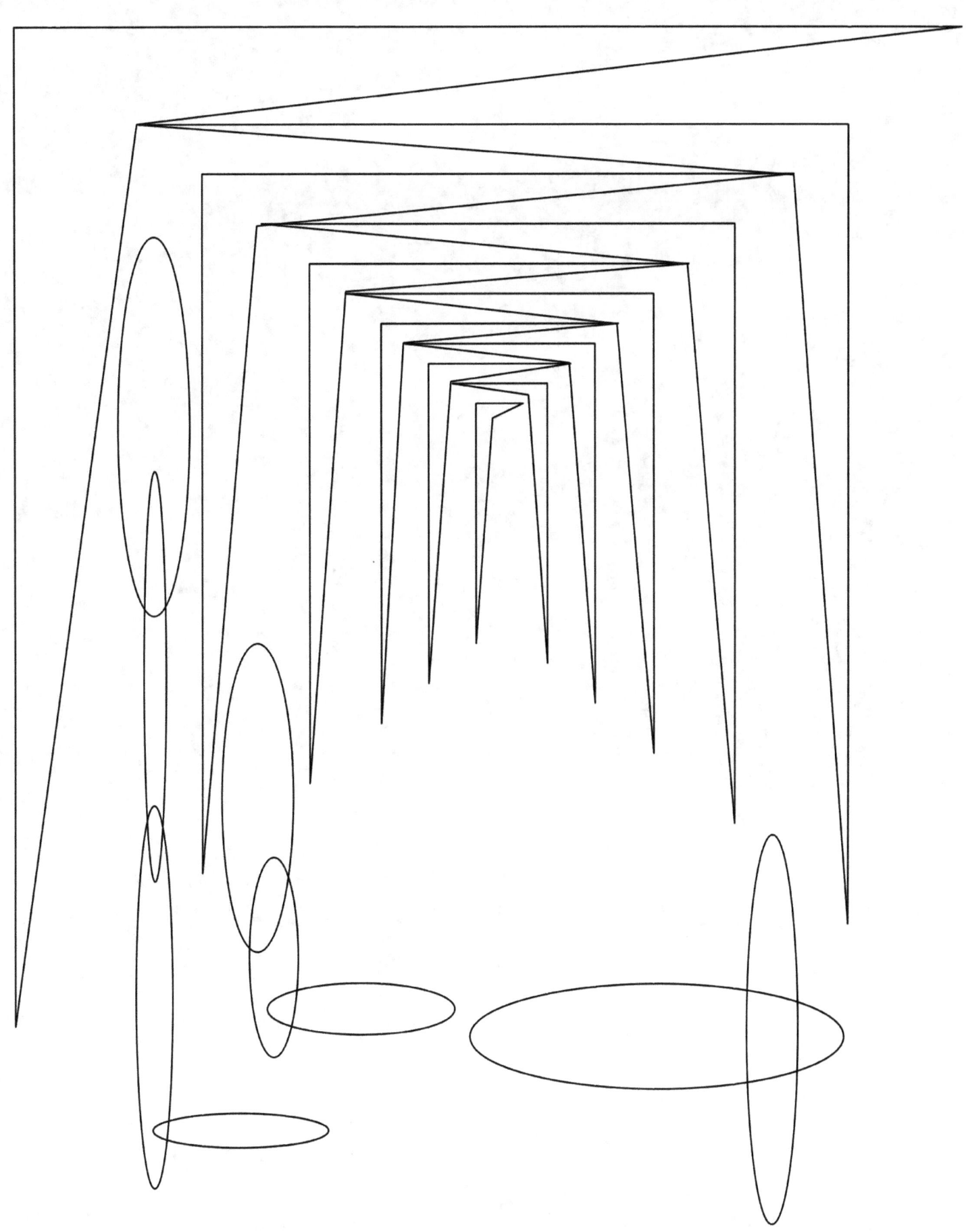

D# 37

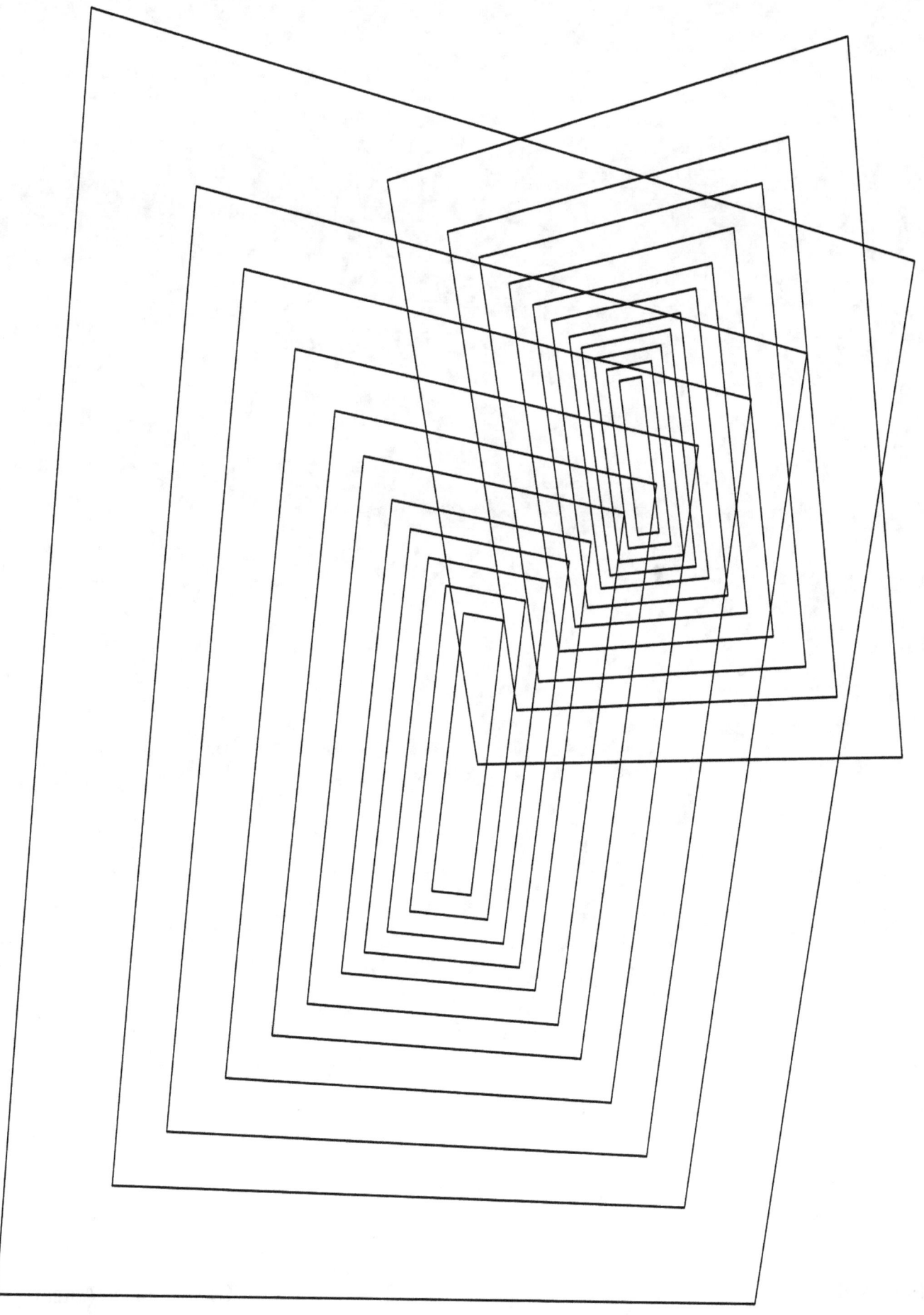

D# 66

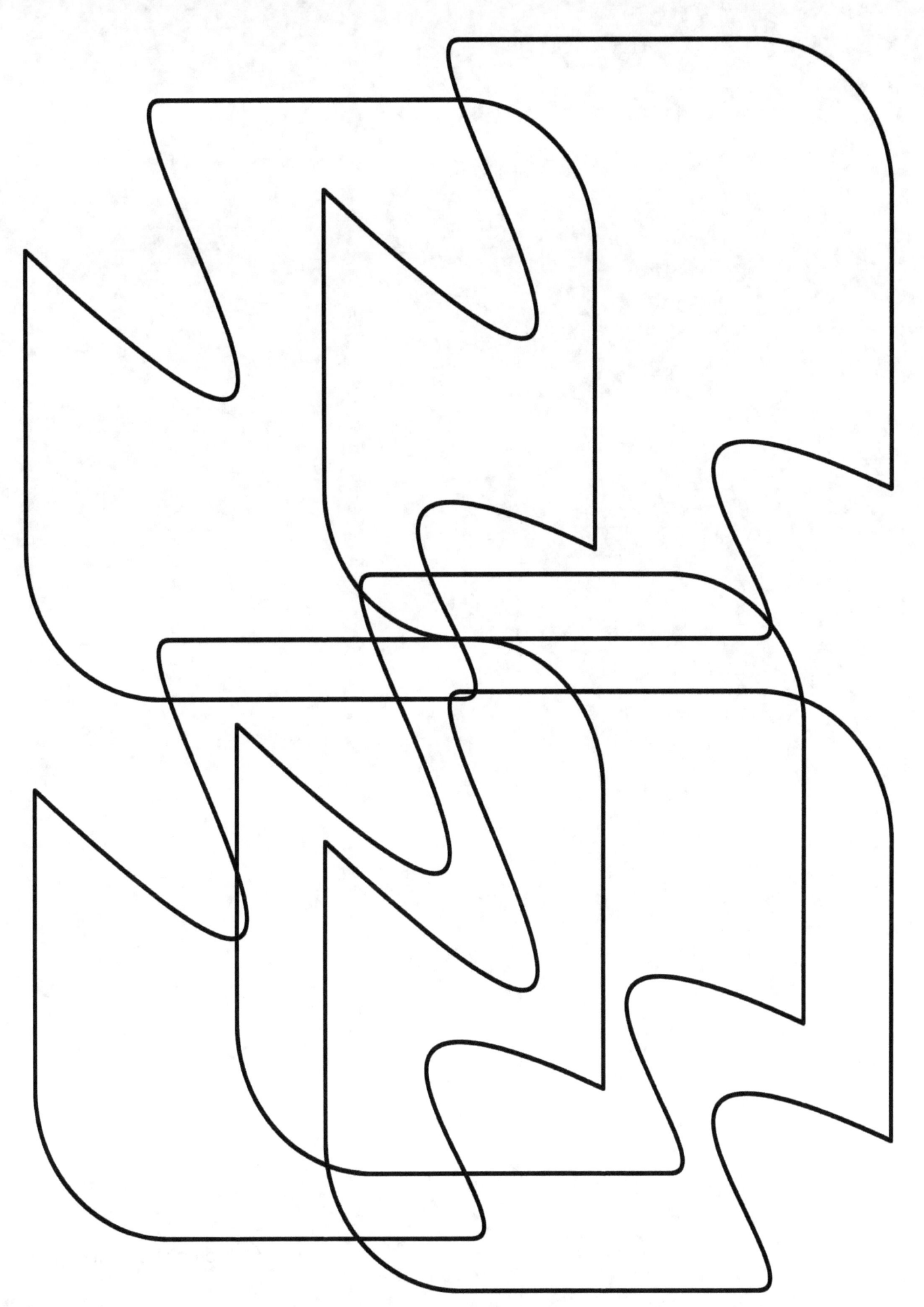

D# 39

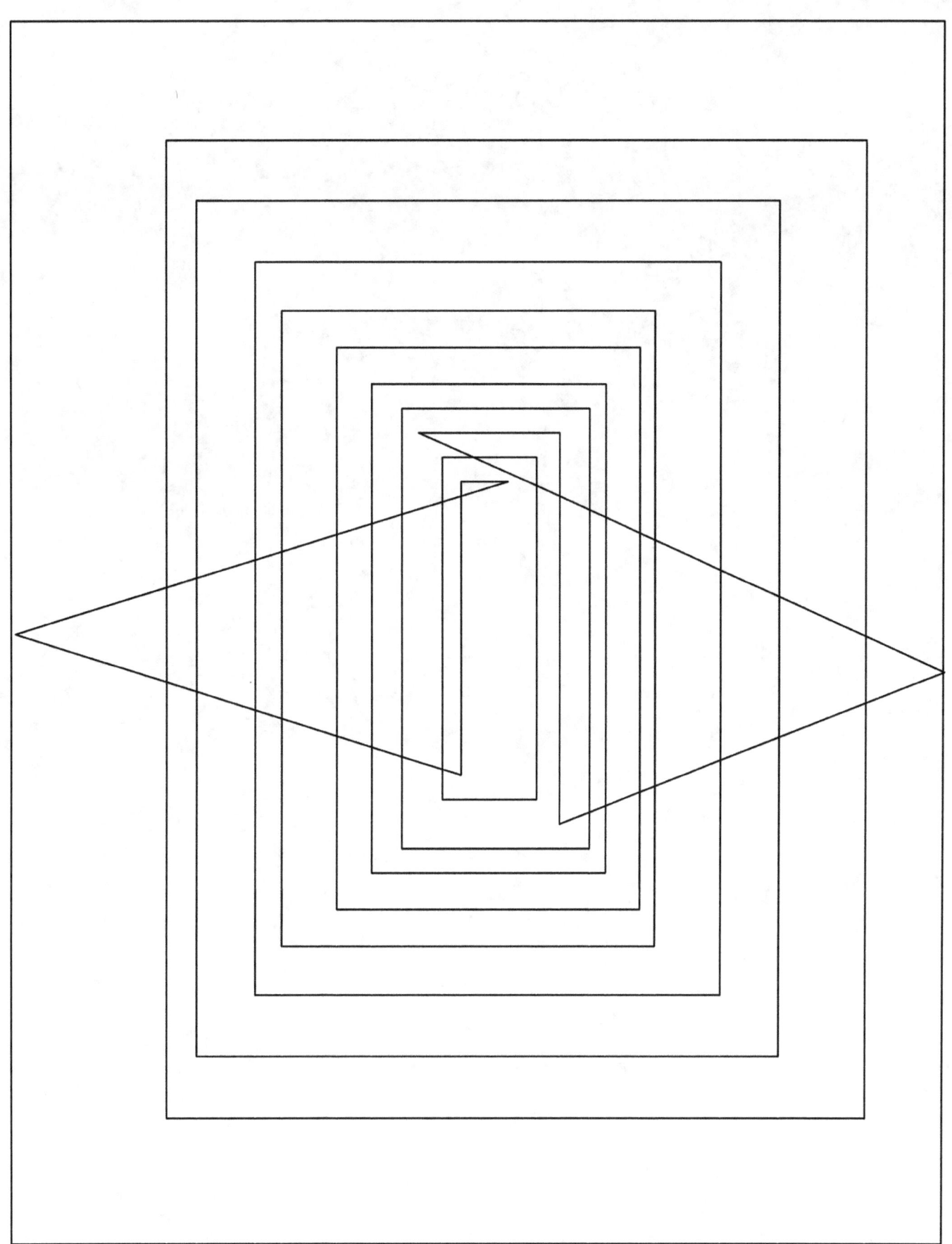

D# 41

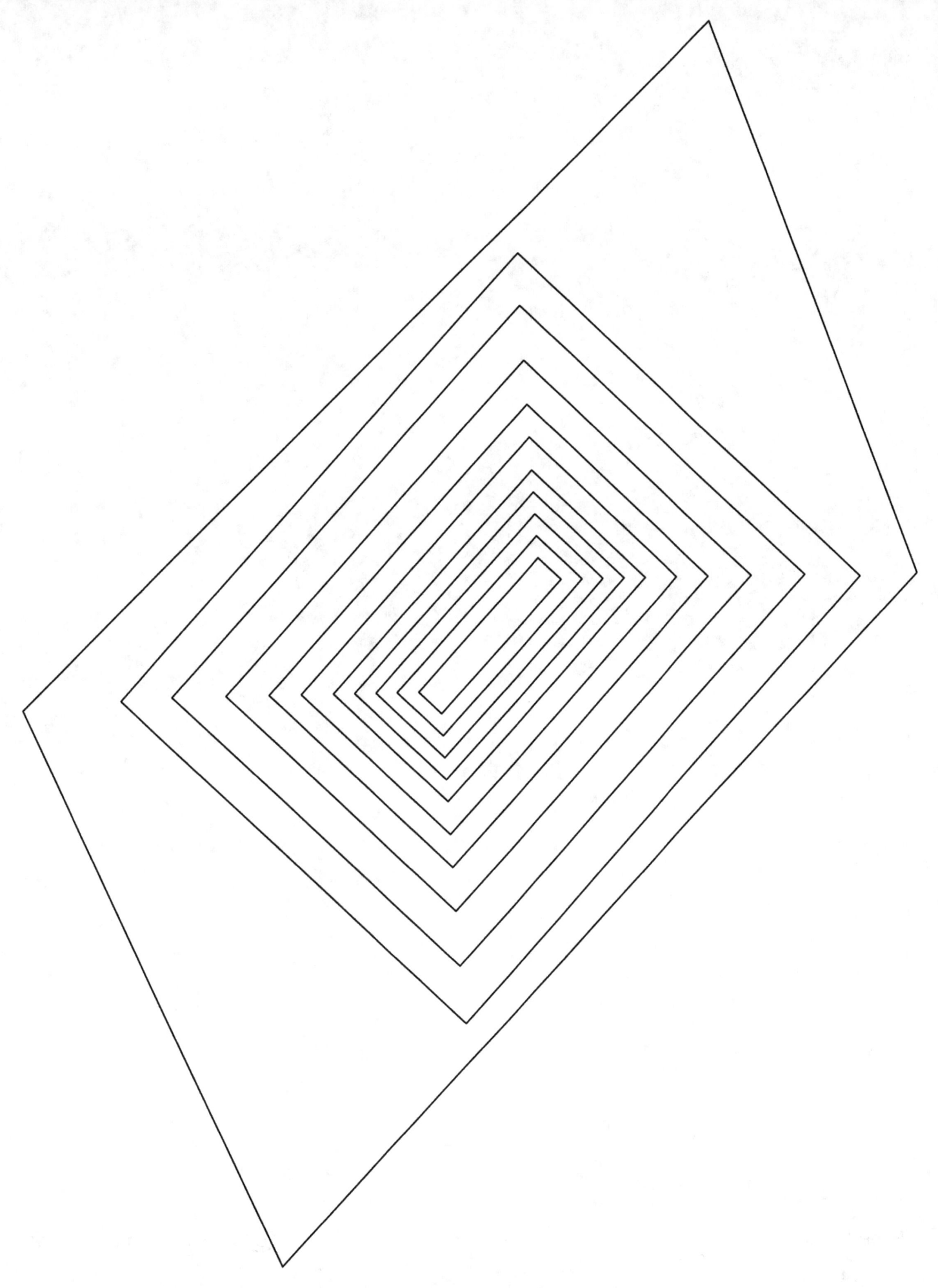

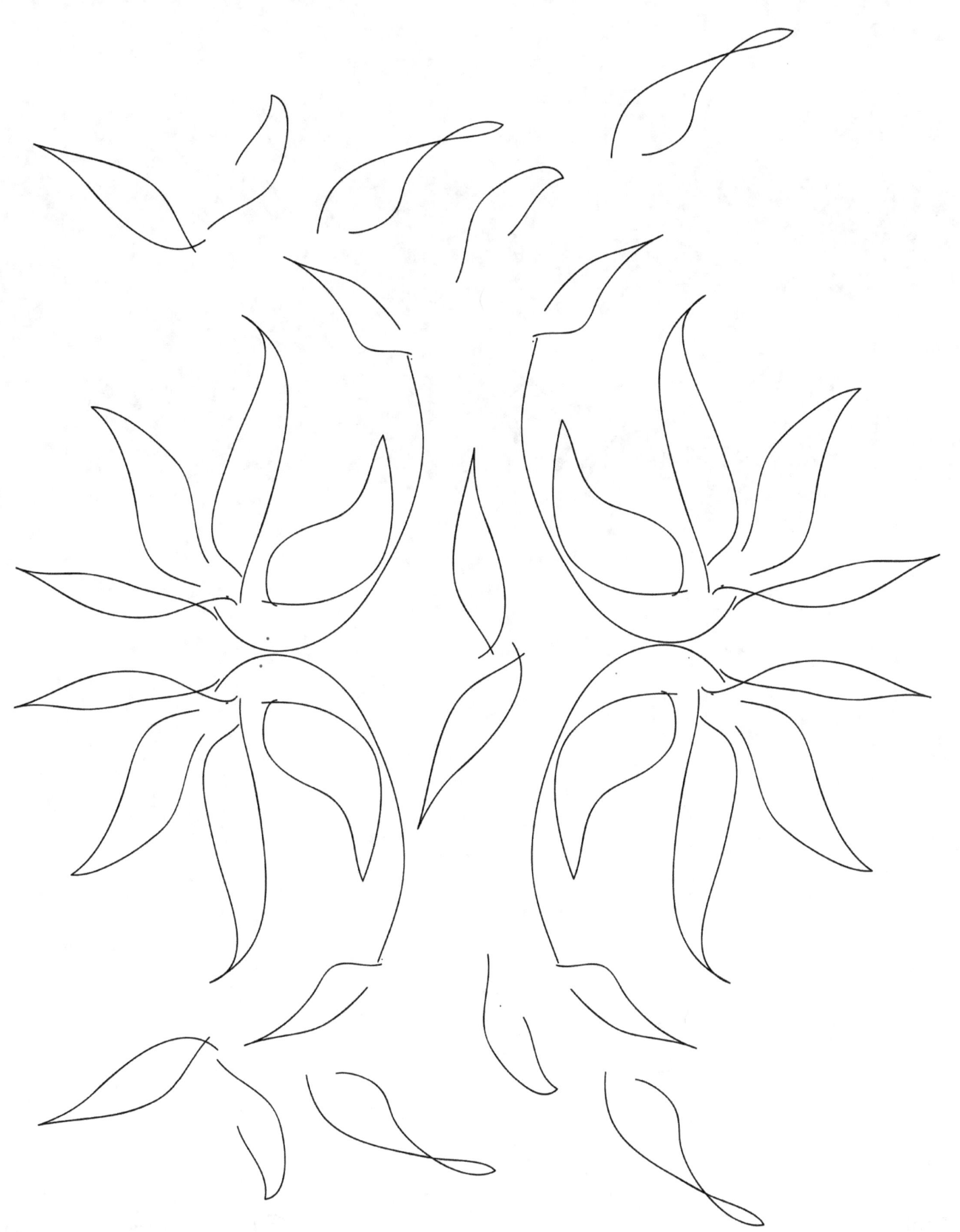

D# 252

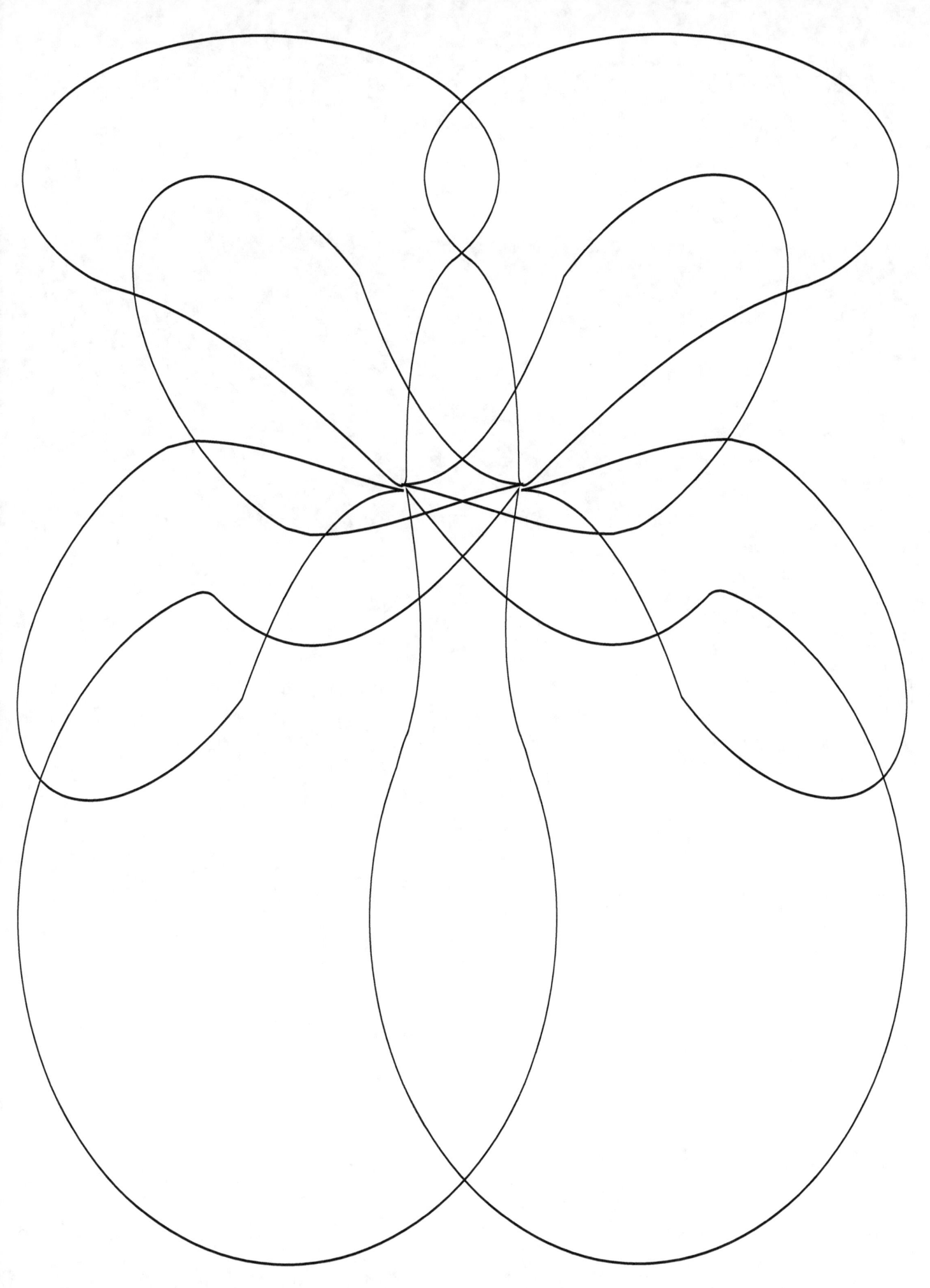

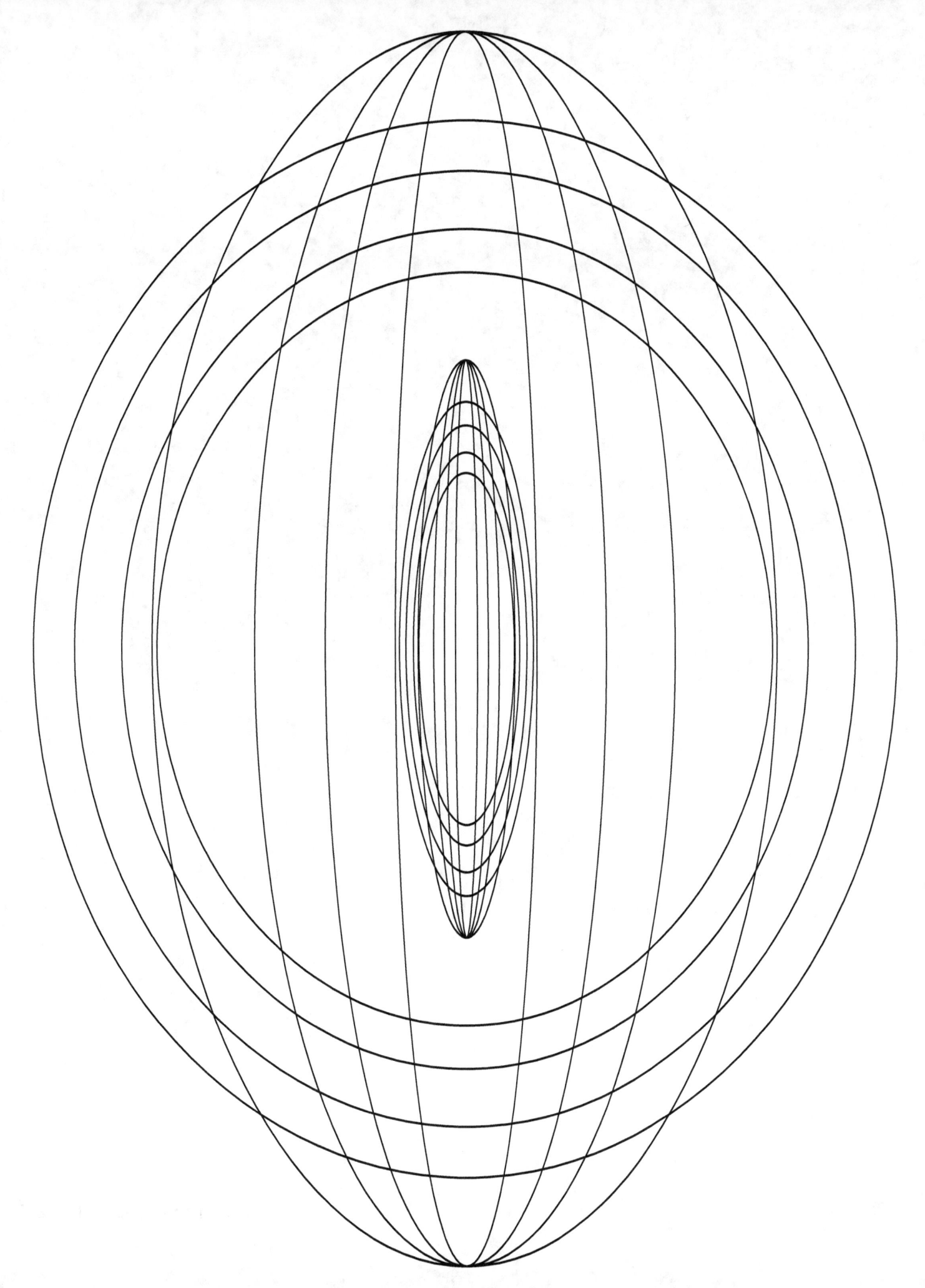

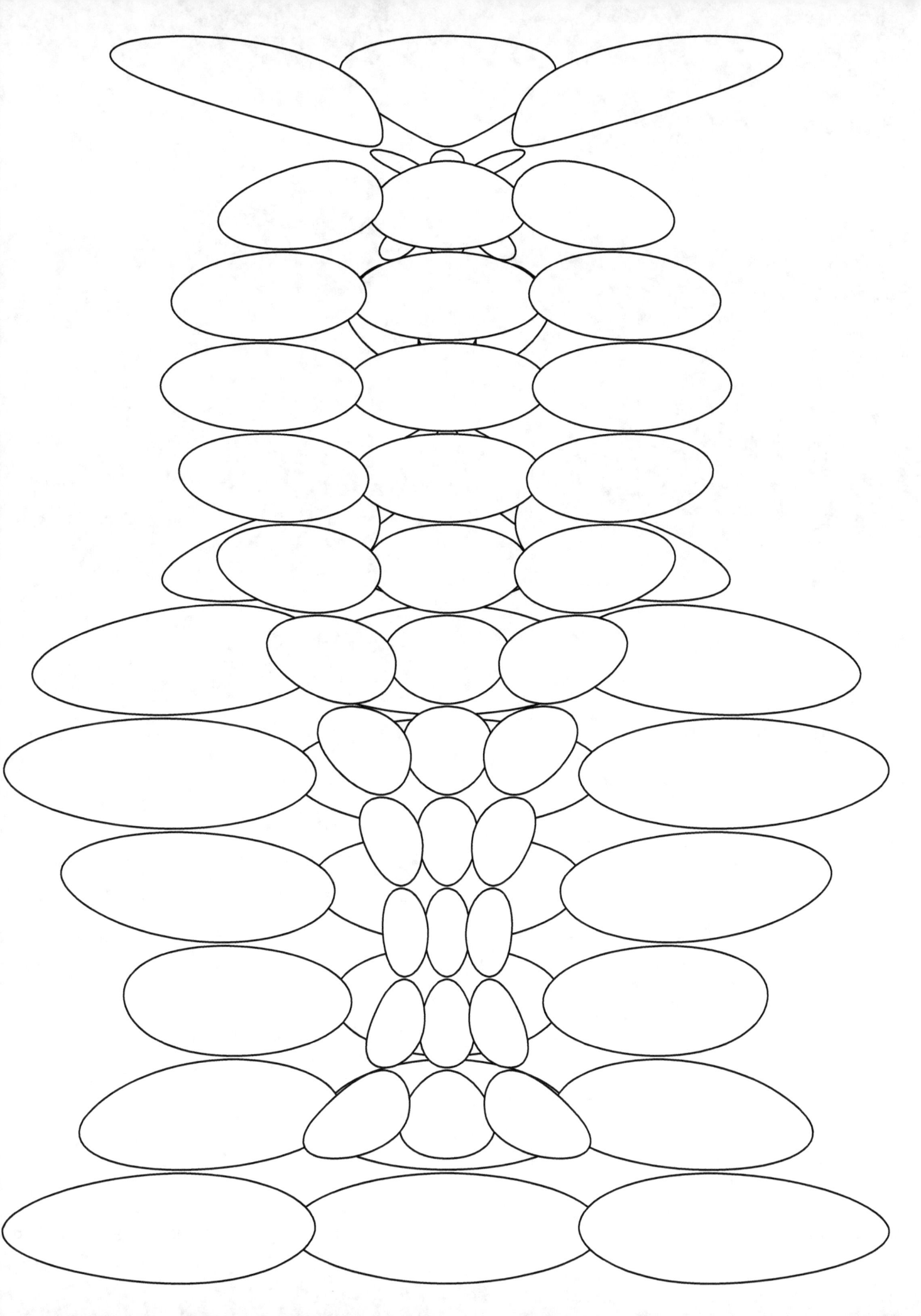

D# 185

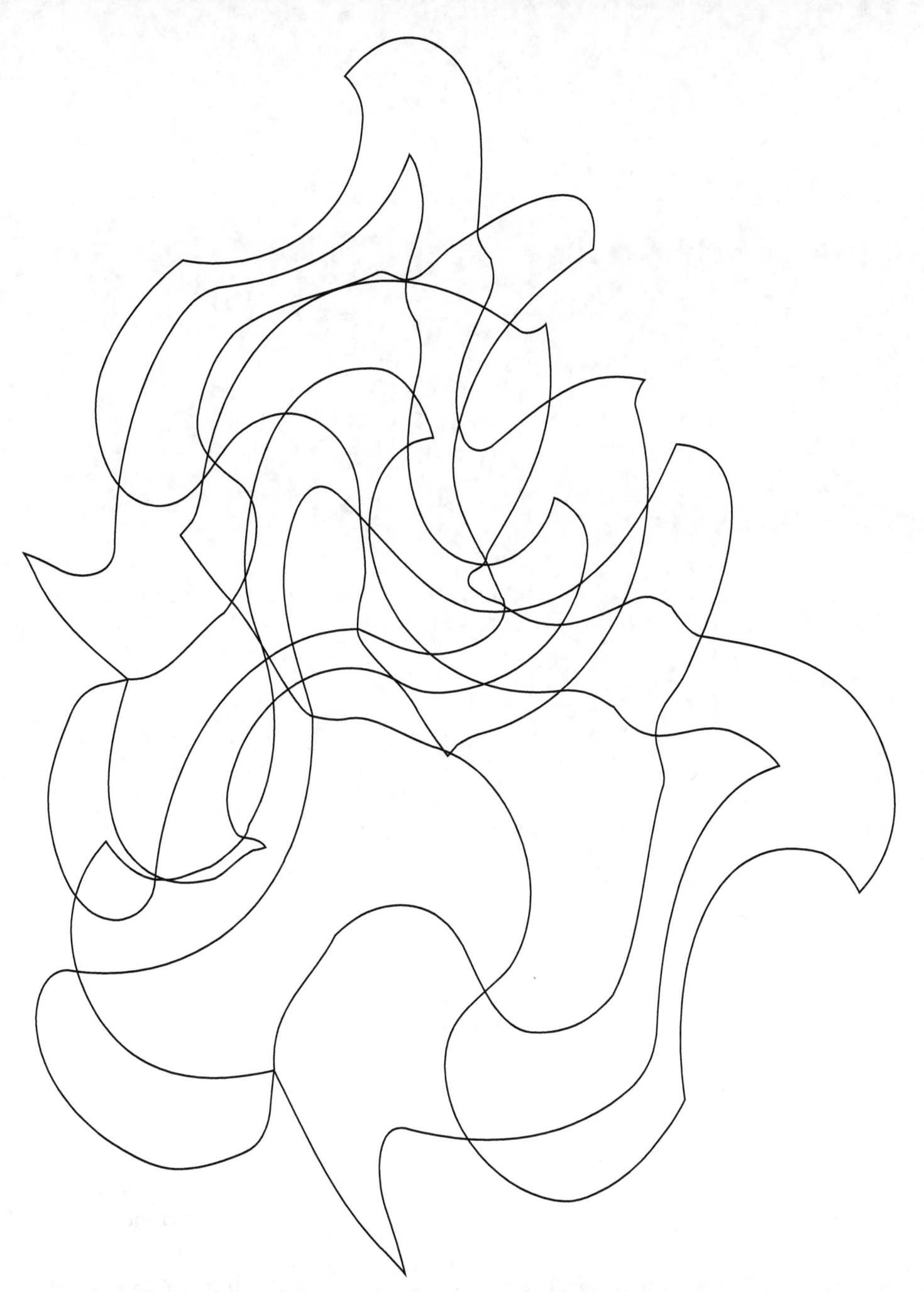

D# 45

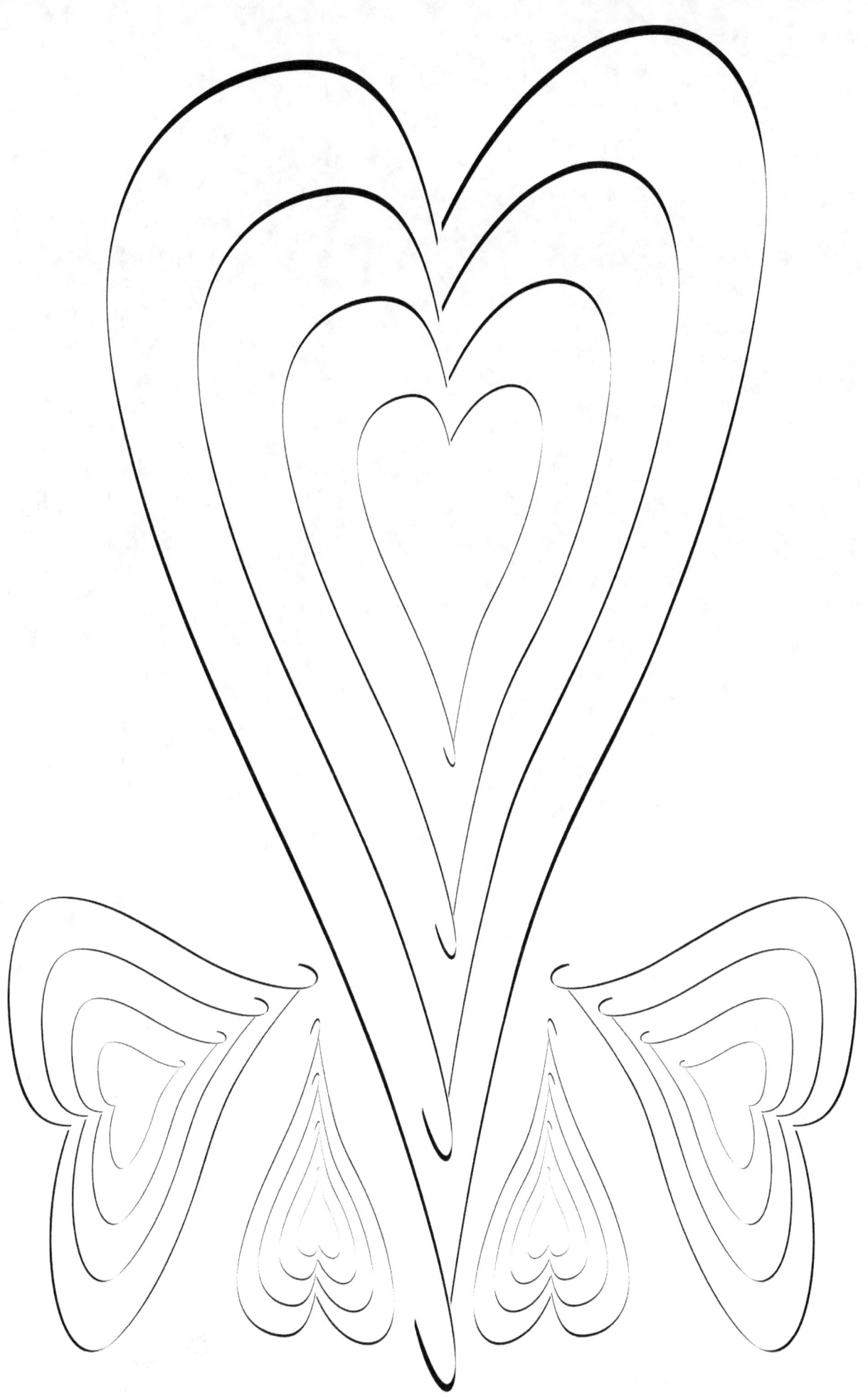

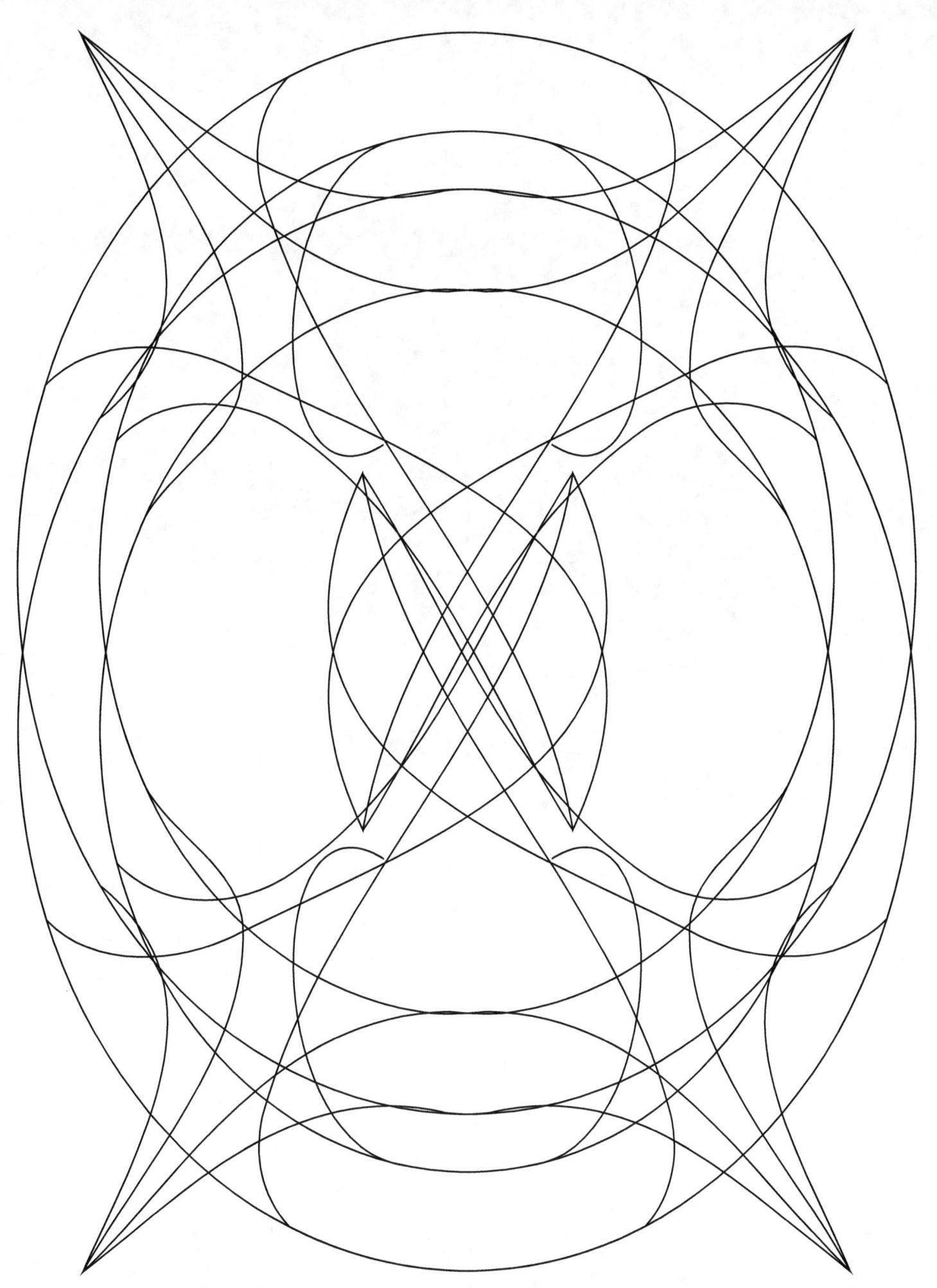

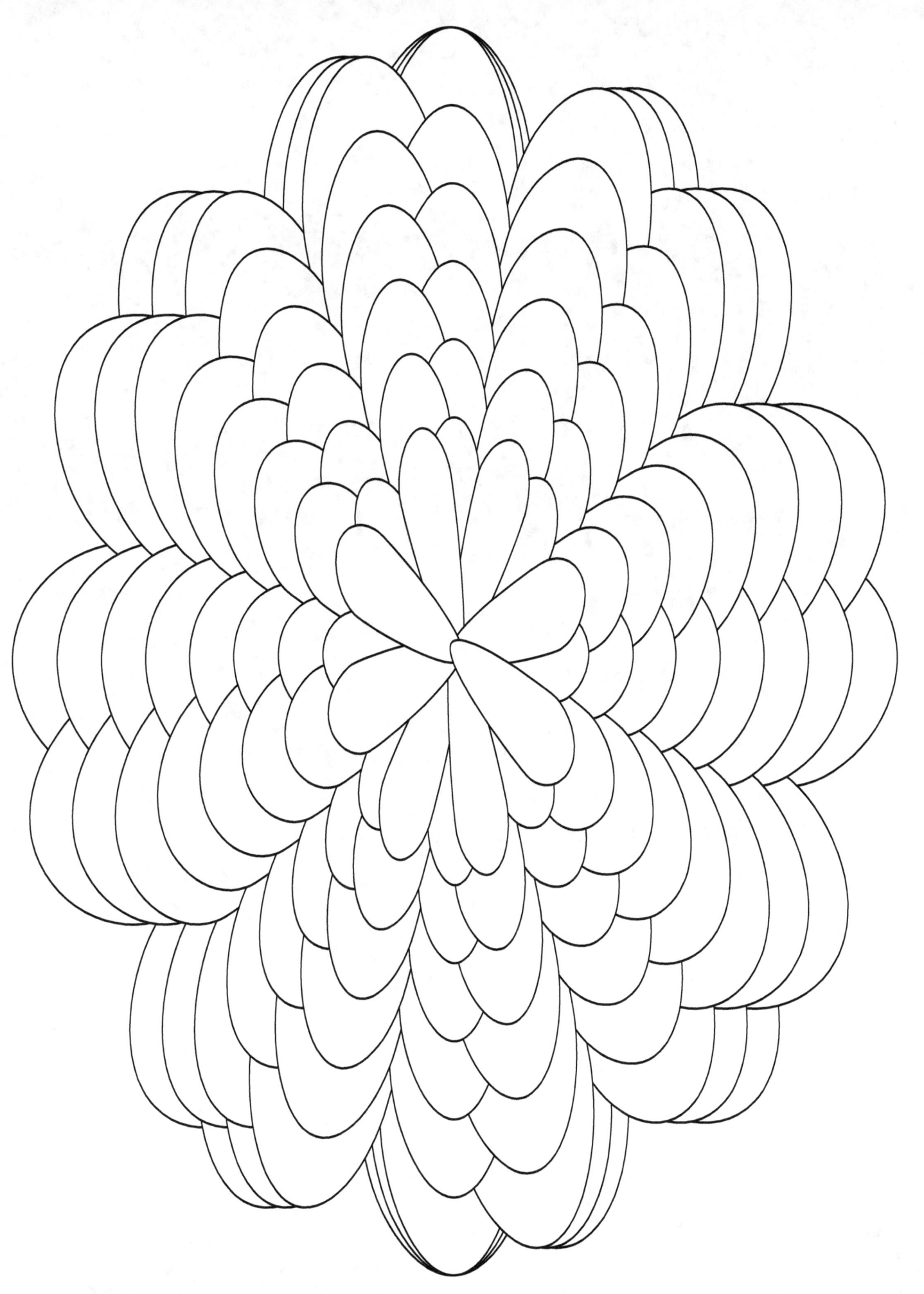

D# 55

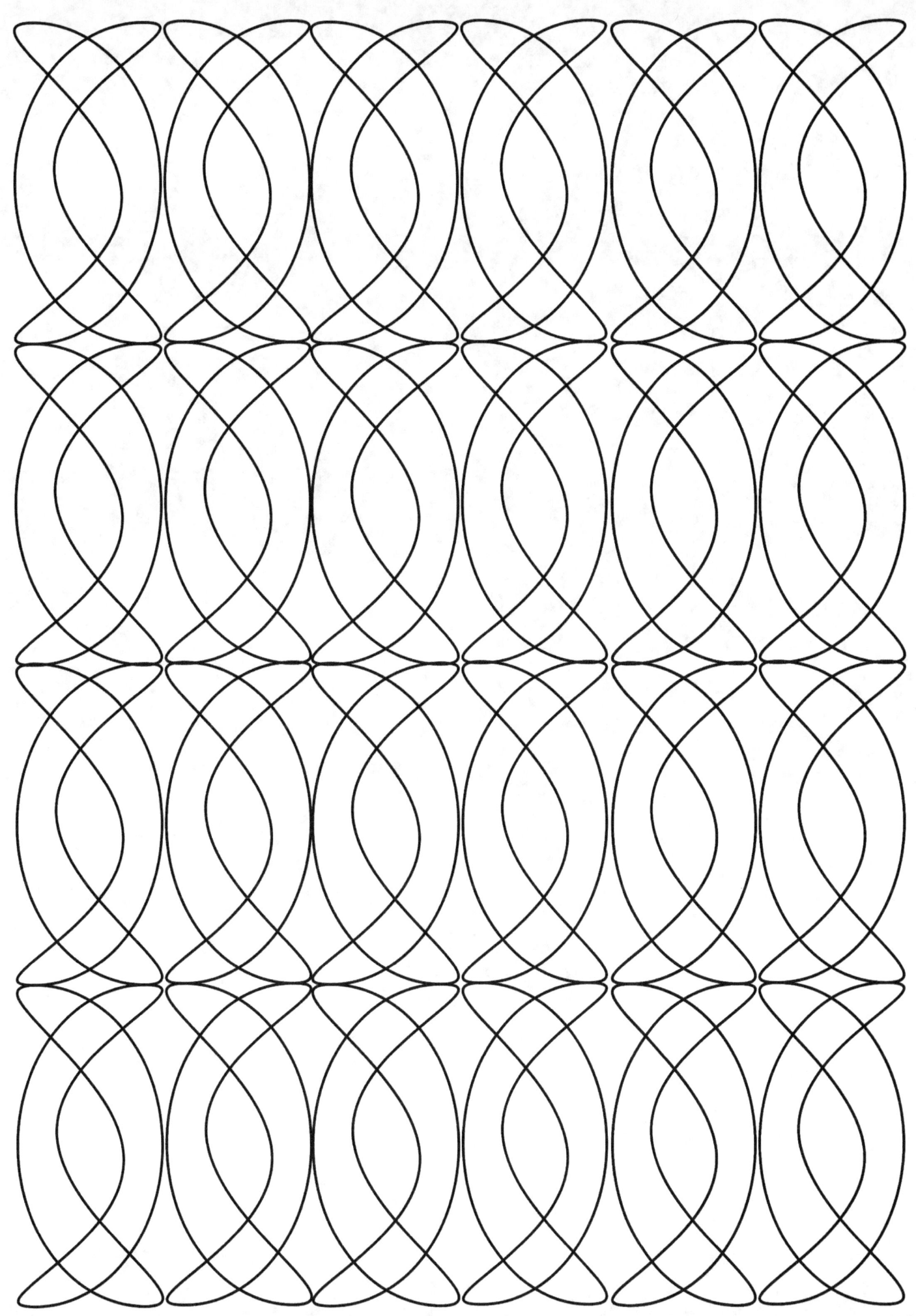

D# 276

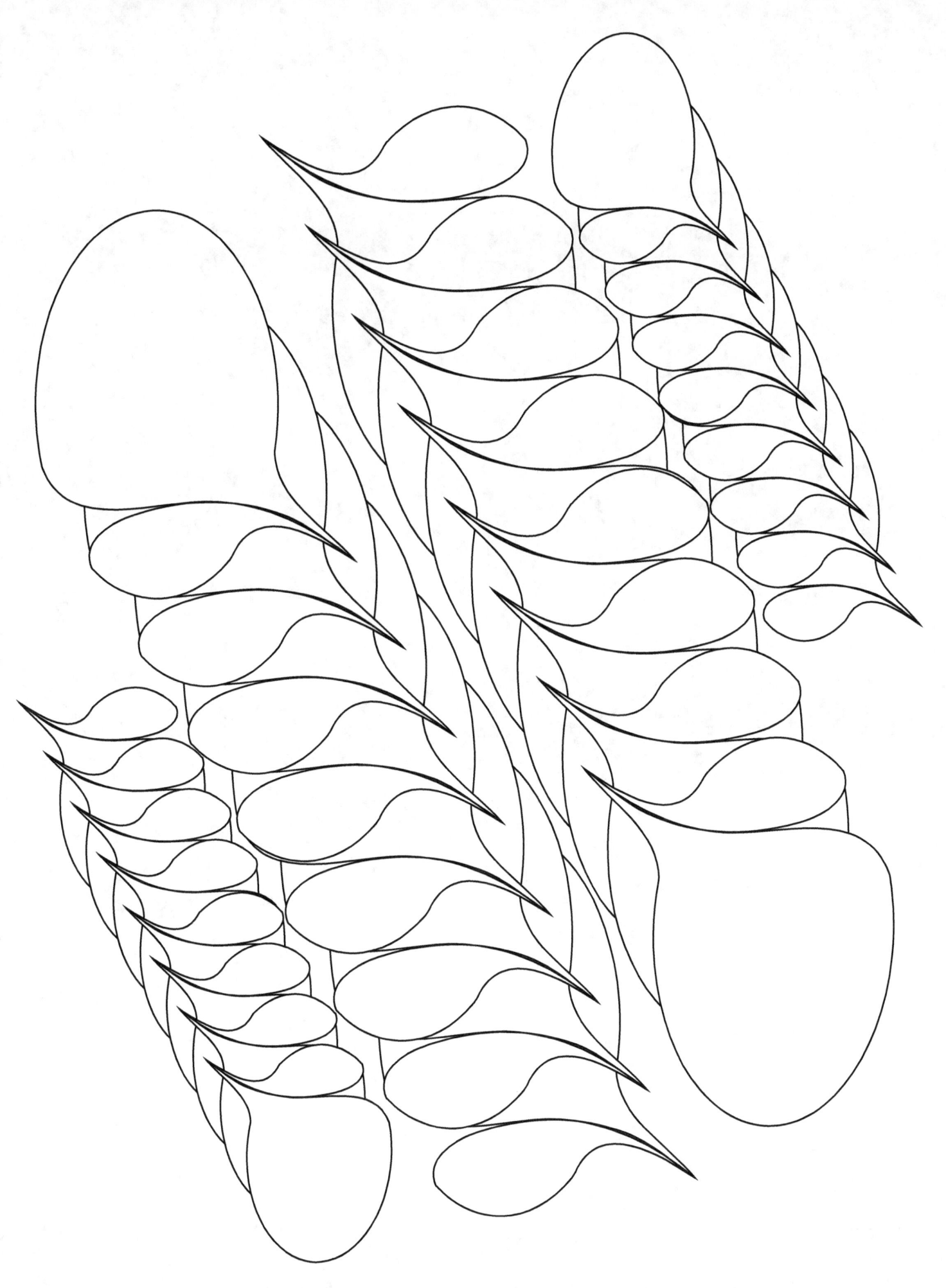

D# 240

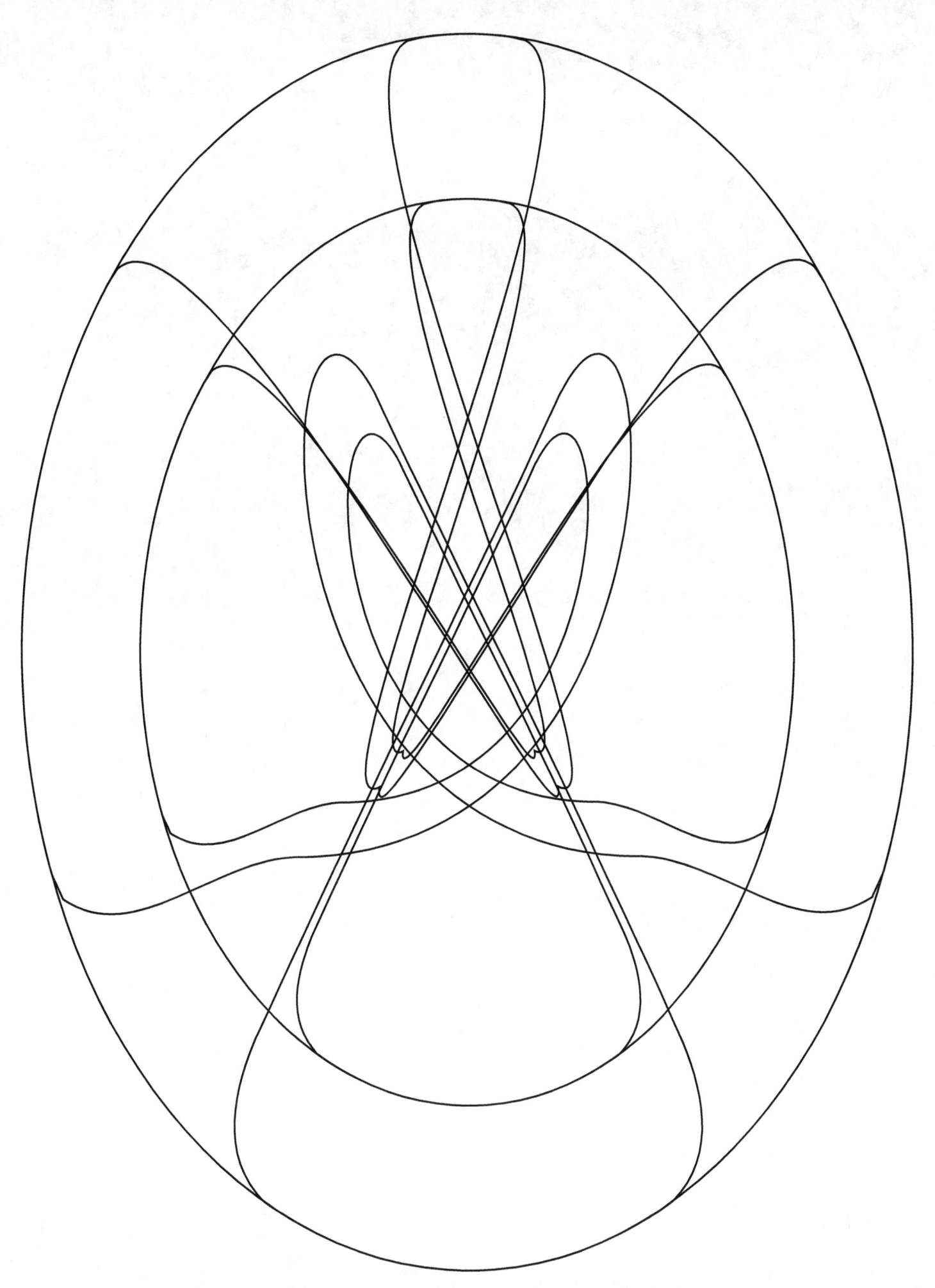

D# 233

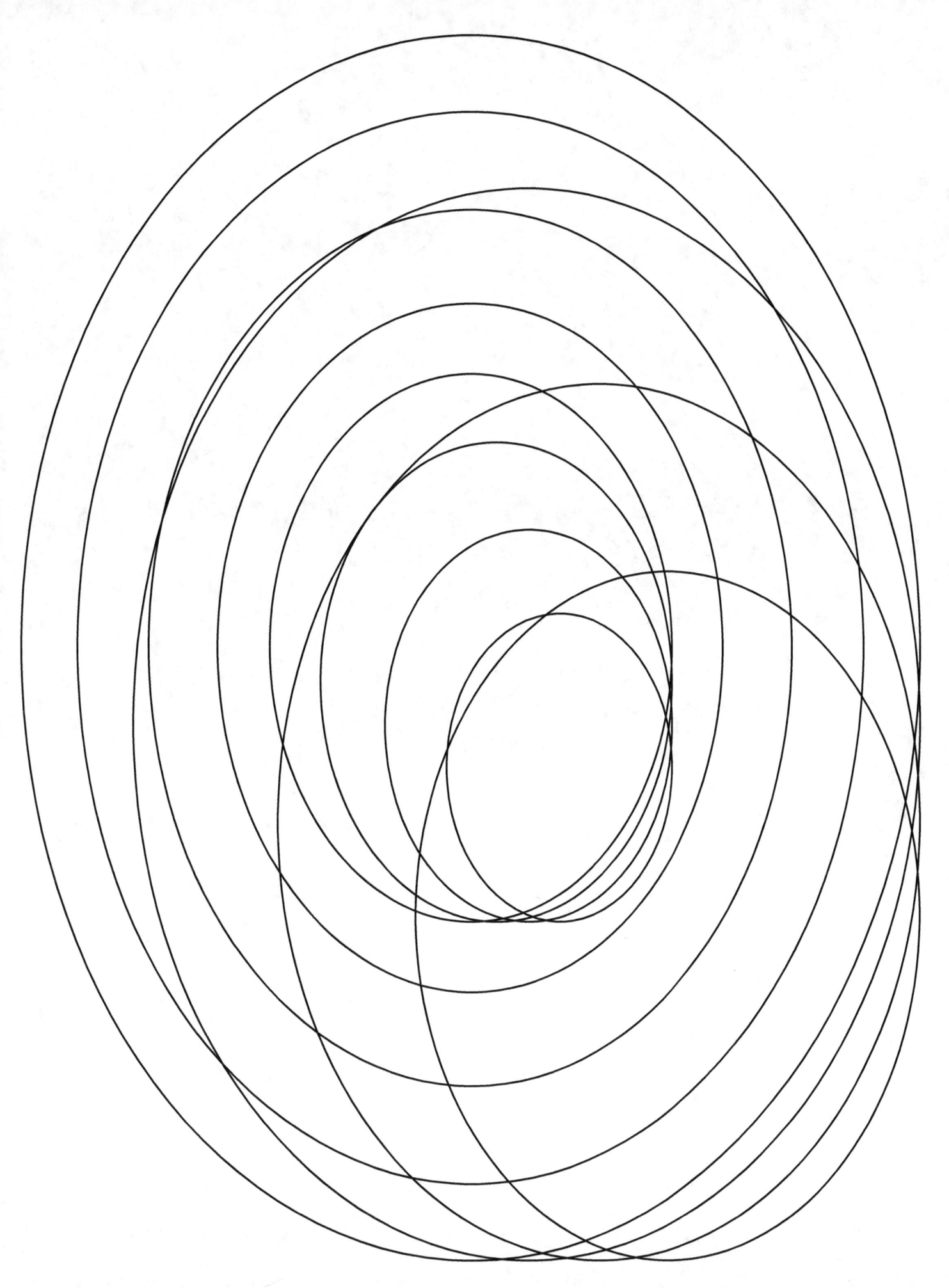

D# 83

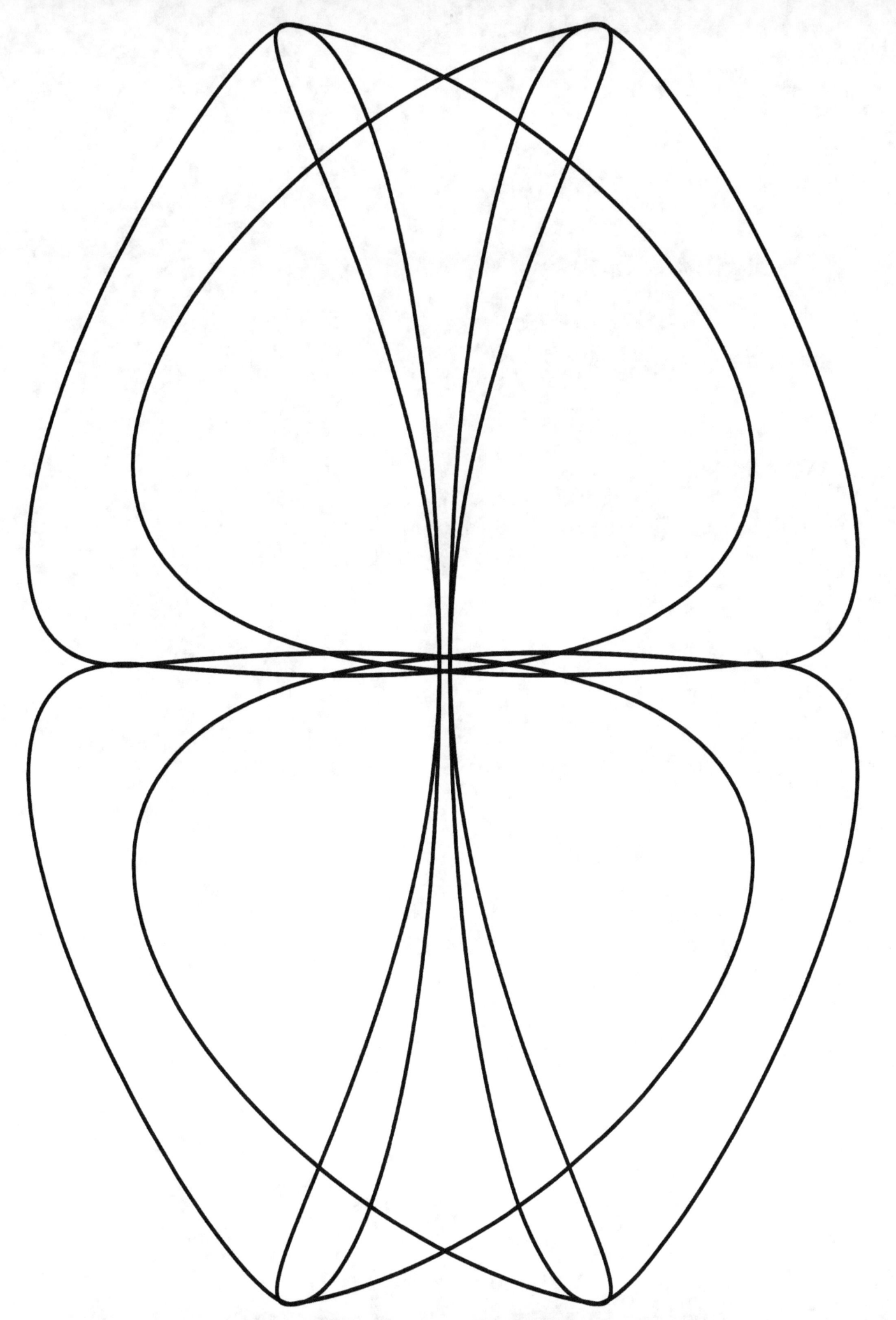